BROMYARD'S INTERESTING STREETS

BY

CHARLES GORDON CLARK

MA, BSc

Published by

BROMYARD AND DISTRICT LOCAL HISTORY SOCIETY
5 SHERFORD STREET, BROMYARD, HEREFORDSHIRE HR7 4DL
Telephone 01885 488755
Registered Charity No 1051572 Founded in 1966

e-mail: bromyardhistory@btconnect.com
www.bromyardhistorysociety.org.uk

First published February 2018

Copyright © Charles Gordon Clark 2018

The right of Charles Gordon Clark to be identified as the author of this work has been asserted by him in accordance with the Copyright, Designs and Patents Act, 1988.

All rights reserved. No part of this publication may be reproduced, stored in a retrieval system or transmitted, in any form or by any means, electronic, mechanical, photocopying, recording or otherwise, without the prior permission, in writing of the publisher.

This book is sold subject to the condition that it shall not, by way of trade or otherwise, be lent, re-sold, hired out, or otherwise circulated without the publisher's prior consent in any form of binding or cover other than that in which it is published and without a similar condition being imposed on the subsequent purchaser.

All photographs are copyright of Bromyard and District Local History Society.

Printed and bound by CreateSpace

ISBN:978-1-978-47096-5

DEDICATED TO

PHYLLIS WILLIAMS

THE DOYENNE OF

BROMYARD STUDIES

BROMYARD'S INTERESTING STREETS

INTRODUCTION

Bromyard is not Anytown, U.K.; although perhaps nowhere is. After living here for six years, and visiting it for a dozen years before, I have my own list of Bromyard's excellences. In no particular order there are the bells of the parish church, recently added to and frequently rung, to the delight of those like me who live within earshot. Then there are the remarkable Christmas lights, surely the best south of Blackpool, serviced by a platoon of dedicated enthusiasts and helped along by collections of small coins throughout the year. Next, the most remarkable and imaginative number of festivals. Then the Bromyard Downs, and Stockings Meadow, with their remarkable flora of meadow plants. Last, and without which this collection of facts could not have been made, the Local History Society. When we were planning to move to Bromyard my daughter said that the first thing I must do was to join the Society. How right she was! Not just the best club in town on a Thursday, a Friday or a Saturday morning, but outstanding among all such societies across the kingdom for the collection of archives, the facilities for research, and the range of publications to which this is a humble addition.

Of course the town has its own particular history, not quite like that of any other. An Anglo-Saxon *monasterium*, not a monastery but a minster, a mission station for north east Herefordshire before there was such a county; then established as a town by Bishop Richard de Capella of Hereford in the 1120s, along with Leominster and Ledbury, at a time when all over Europe this was the surest way to economic development. Burgage plots, long and narrow, many surviving to this day, a market, free citizens, what was not to admire in this pattern. Apart from the bishop, no overbearing lord, no castle, no abbey.

The crises of the Black Death in the 14th, the Reformation in the 16th and the Civil War in the 17th centuries seem to have left Bromyard fairly untouched, but something of a backwater; Leominster and Ledbury grew faster and were earlier served by a railway in the 19th century. And when the railway came it linked Bromyard not with Hereford, the county town, but with Worcester, and eventually with Leominster; people began to date their letters from "Bromyard, Worcester". Would things have been different if it had found itself on the direct line from Worcester to Hereford? It seems from the road numbering of the early 20th century that Bromyard was regarded as being on the direct road between these two county and cathedral towns, as well as what it had always been, on the direct road from London and Oxford to the Welsh coast at Aberystwyth. Industry came slowly and fitfully, though in a distinguished manner with the first Morgan motor car, and is now in a familiar early 21st century pattern of having a number of estates of light industry.

These essays on the streets began when my daughter and son-in-law asked for something to publicise the unfortunate state of the former magistrates' court, later library, opposite their house in Church Street. Someone at the History Society suggested an article on the road in "*Off the Record*", the town's monthly magazine. It seemed popular enough to make a series, and this is what these essays originally were.

Thanks to all who helped with them, especially the Publications Committee of the BDLHS who provided the photographs and have overseen the process of turning my text into a professional looking book; also of course to Phyllis Williams and the other pioneers of a professional approach to Bromyard's history.

Other thanks are due to Denis Teal on Frog Lane, Charles Hopkinson on Linton Lane, Peter Gilbert and David Tinton on Rowberry Street, and the late Keith Handley on Firs Lane.

CHARLES GORDON CLARK, 2018.

CONTENTS

1. CHURCH STREET — 5
2. SHERFORD STREET — 11
3. ROWBERRY STREET — 15
4. MARKET SQUARE — 21
5. BROAD STREET — 26
6. FROG LANE — 33
7. PUMP STREET AND TOWER HILL — 37
8. HIGH STREET — 40
9. NEW ROAD — 48
10. CRUXWELL STREET — 53
11. CHURCH LANE — 61
12. OLD ROAD — 65
13. TENBURY ROAD — 69
14. FIRS LANE — 75
15. LINTON LANE — 78

Further Reading — 85

1. CHURCH STREET

It's fitting to begin this series with Church Street, because it is, along with Sherford Street, the original street of the town. This is shown by the *Red Book*, a document of about 1285 drawn up for the Bishops of Hereford showing, basically, how much money they could screw out of the inhabitants of the diocese. They had founded Bromyard, along with Leominster, Ross, and Ledbury, probably in the 1120s, on one of their principal manors. Founding towns was the way to economic development just then. In the list of burgesses in the *Red Book*, Church and Sherford Street are called *vicus vetus*, the old street, and Broad and High Street *vicus novus*,[1] the new street. So the town had prospered in its first century and a half, and more than doubled in size.

None of the existing buildings in Church Street of course are so old; but several houses have their original long narrow "burgess plot" whose occupant for centuries had a right to practise a trade in the town and share in its governance. No. 23 is a good example, having a width to the street of 25 feet and 2 inches, which is just over a statute perch and a half, and a length of 130 feet, about 8 perches. Some of the woodwork inside is 17th century, perhaps dating from when it was an adjunct of the inn next door. This property, now Johnson's, has a frontage of a little over three perches, so was perhaps originally two burgess plots.

It was, as can still be seen, "The Railway Inn" when it was last licensed premises. But it had several earlier names, Crown Inn in 1811, then Bell Inn, then Barley Mow, then in 1835 Masons's Arms when the landlord was a stone mason, changing to Carrier's Arms by 1861 when that was the other profession of the landlord. It only changed to its last name when the railway and station came further down the road. On the bow window is still engraved the name and

---

[1] It seems like *lèse-majesté* to correct Phyllis Williams, who calls the streets *Vico Veteri* and *Vico Novo*, but these forms follow the Latin preposition *in*; without that the nominative forms were as I give them.

"Bar"; on the other ground floor window "Commercial" - readers of Trollope's novels will remember that commercial travellers often had their own rather jealously guarded room in hostelries.

This was not the only inn in the street; nearer the church at different times in the 18th century were the Red Lion and the Adam and Eve.

CHURCH STREET

At the Market Place end was another Bell Inn which had earlier been the Three Horseshoes when the beer retailer was also a blacksmith. That had its licence revoked in 1936 as being redundant, at the time when the *News and Record* reckoned that there was a pub in Bromyard for every 98 inhabitants! But there's still a name plaque on the Old Bell Inn.

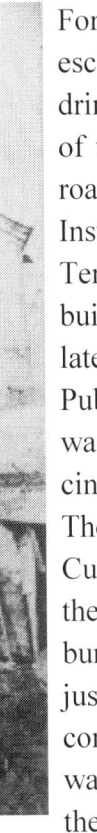

For those who eschewed the demon drink, at the north end of the east side of the road a Working Men's Institute and Temperance Hall was built in 1859 which later became the Public Hall. In 1922 it was fitted out as a cinema ("the Electric Theatre") by Edward Cuff, the landlord of the Falcon, but it was burnt down in 1931 just as "talkies" were coming in; the site was redeveloped with the present house.

BURNT ELECTRIC THEATRE

There are several particularly notable buildings in the street. Pride of place nowadays must go to the Post Office, because it is still serving the purpose for which it was built in 1911, unlike what has happened in so many towns, where the post office has slunk inside some other store.

The architect was Herbert Skyrme (1871-1944), who also designed the lychgate at Bishop's Frome church and did much other work across the county, but this striking building is probably his masterpiece.

Skyrme was a former pupil of F. R. Kempson (1838-1923), the architect of parts of both Bishop's Frome and Stoke Lacy churches. He is represented in Church Street by the larger, north, part of the former Grammar School (now Hydro-logic). The southern part had

THE POST OFFICE

been rebuilt by the Goldsmiths' Company, one of the City of London livery companies, in 1835. The grammar school (for boys only) had been part of the parish outreach since before the Reformation, hence its position next to the churchyard. The income which kept it up was added to in 1656 by a legacy from the Bromyard born John Perrin, a

London alderman and member of the Goldsmiths' Company, hence their subsequent interest.

The sad group of buildings on the east side of Church Street will be remembered by many Bromyardians as the Library, and before that as the Youth Club and Resource Centre. It was bought by the County Council when the court closed at the end of 1987 as centralising services came in. The right hand portion was built in 1862-3 for £600 as the Magistrates' Court on land bought for £26 14s. and possibly a greenfield site before that. A Police Station was added next door in a similar style in 1875. The architect was William Chick (1829-92), the county surveyor for many years. He was probably influenced by Kempson in the design.

With its striking combination of local Old Red Sandstone (actually yellow!) with oolitic limestone dressings and patterned brickwork they are a notable pair of buildings which should be preserved. But they are in a sad state of decay. It is to be hoped that the present owners do not wish them to get so far gone that they can demolish them.

The earlier Court House was the nearby Dumbleton Hall, named after the Domulton family of Brockhampton who had a town house there in the later Middle Ages. The present building is a 17th century house remodelled twice in the 19th century after the Manorial Court moved there in the early 19th century. When that ancient institution lapsed the Petty Sessions or Magistrates' Court was held there. In the 1860s the magistrates heard cases of petty crime and other business in the new building every Monday at 1 p.m.; in the 1870s every other Monday at 11 a.m. Later on, the County Court, for civil cases not involving much money, was held there twice monthly, and so were occasional coroner's courts.

No. 4 faces boldly down the street: the Bible House, whose name is misleading. It comes from the Bibble brook, itself perhaps derived from the Latin for *to drink*, which used to run across the Market

Square. It is supposed to be still noticeable in the cellars of the Crown and Sceptre. It is a rather late timber framed house if the inscribed date 1685 refers to the whole building; but it may be that of additions, and there are more from the 18th and 19th centuries.

The corruption of a name to a familiar religious word is also seen in Brockhampton Park, where "Holy Bank" was originally *Howley*, from Anglo-Saxon words meaning "ridge where the land falls sharply". It had become "Holly Bank" until, according to Phyllis Williams, Colonel Lutley insisted on the correct pronunciation, and that then led, quite recently, to the same mutation to a familiar word.

Church Street may be short, but it is filled with Bromyard's history.

2. SHERFORD STREET

Sherford Street, as said above, is part of the first street laid out in the town in the 1120s, the *vicus vetus* of the Red Book. It leads up from the *short ford* (Schordesford in 1341) where Petty (*little*) Bridge replaced it on the ancient Worcester to Leominster road at some unknown date. The road was widened at Petty Bridge in 1776, and the present bridge was built in 1810.

PETTY BRIDGE, LATE 19TH CENTURY

The most prominent building is Sherford House of about 1770, perhaps built as a dower or town house to Brockhampton House, and like that designed by Thomas Farnolls Pritchard of Shrewsbury. The bricks are laid in Flemish Bond (alternately 'stretcher', long, and 'header', short), as in later and smaller buildings in the road. The Girls' High School, run by the Wesleyans, moved there from what's now Pettifer's hardware shop in 1898, and closed in 1906. That year it had thirty pupils, half of them boarders. In 1909 it became for three years St. Joseph's Convent, with a Community of Sisters of Providence, who also had a short-lived house in Ledbury. That year "Shrove Tuesday was kept as Shrove Tuesday and not just pancake day"! Then for six months in 1914 it was St. Mary's Priory, a convent of Olivetan Benedictine nuns, but apparently this was too much for very Protestant Bromyard.

At the top of the road next to the Post Office yard is the premises of the Bromyard and District Local History Society (BDLHS). The society was founded in 1966 and by 1999 badly needed a large permanent home for its extensive archive and more space for equipment, a library, and research facilities generally. In that year the two storey building erected in 1913 as a warehouse for Addyman's grocery shop in the Square came on the market. It was bought with "a combination of Society funds, loans from members and a small grant from the Town Council", and a grant for adaptation was obtained from the Heritage Lottery Fund. Much of the conversion was done by working parties of members and the building opened in 2003.

Below it, the Crown and Sceptre is late 18th or early 19th century, but partly built round an earlier building, as there are beams inside which James Tonkin in his chapter on "Houses of Bromyard" in the 1970 *"Bromyard, A Local History"*(see Further Reading), thought 17th century. He pointed out "the fine glazing bars of the type usually found in the better building".

Opposite, no. 10, The Steps, is converted from the old vinegar factory (the Old Malt House), which had probably been purpose-built for that, re-using big timbers from an older property. The top storey has crucks designed to give head room for storing the barley for fermenting into malt. Mr. Thursby the printer and stationer in the Market Square had his printing press there in the 1920s.

The Chapel was originally built by Presbyterians in 1701/2. They had been licensed to have a Meeting House in 1672, in John Bond's house, and the tradition is the site was that of the later chapel. It is in a new style for the town, a simple square building with a hipped roof and tall narrow windows; a handsome Doric porch shows the growing self-confidence of Non-conformist or Dissenting congregations. The stone (very pale local Old Red Sandstone, but not red, except at the base plinth, and possibly from Clater Park quarry) is carefully cut and squared. It later became Congregational, and on March 31st 1851 had three services with congregations of 50 in the morning, with 30 in the Sunday School, 31 in the afternoon, and 105 in the evening.

THE CONGREGATIONAL CHAPEL

Before World War 1 it was thriving. It closed for worship in 1971. At the rear is the former manse of 1874.

A careful archaeological survey was carried out by Border Archaeology of Leominster in 2011 before the site and adjoining buildings were redeveloped. This revealed a relatively short lived burial ground that was found to extend both under the Chapel and into the yard outside, indicating that they were burying people under the floor of the chapel whilst it was in use. It has been suggested that the burial ground might slightly predate the chapel. 21 Burials were revealed and some had coffin plates identifying them, all burials dated from the 18th and 19th century.

The Herefordshire magistrates decided in 1843 that Bromyard needed a "Lockuphouse" as there was no dungeon and only two small cells at Dumbleton Hall. So they bought, from John Barneby of Brockhampton, a site next to the chapel, and the County Surveyor, John Gray, designed a proper police station with cells. The classical pediment was presumably to emphasize the high standards delinquents were falling short of. The building became a private residence when the magistrates' court in Church Street was built thirty years later.

LOCK UP CONVERTED TO PRIVATE DWELLING

These buildings backed onto a field called "The Forburys", "in front of the borough". That name has been revived for the newly refurbished group of all these buildings, including the chapel which is doubling as dwelling house and art gallery.

3. ROWBERRY STREET

There are Bromyardians to this day who refer to Rowberry Street as "Back Street", and it is a pity that that name was ever dropped. The road has no connection with Rowberry farm in Bodenham or with anyone of that name. It was "Bowbury Streate" in 1578 when a

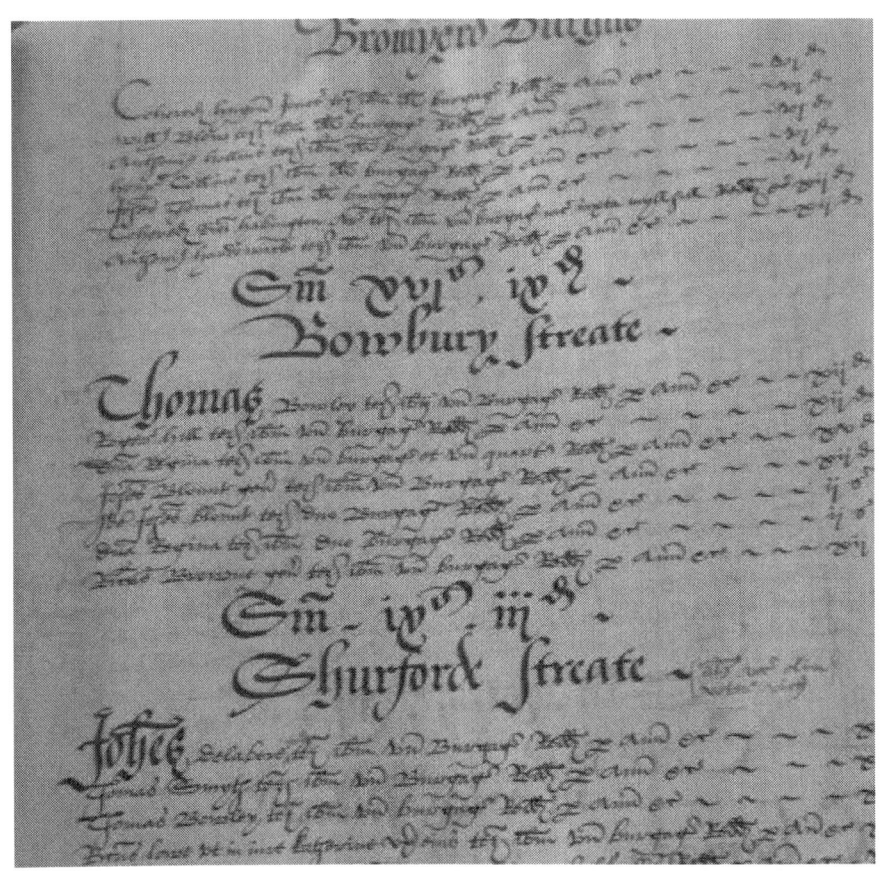

PAGE FROM SWITHUN BUTTERFIELD'S SURVEY OF 1578

survey of Bromyard was made for Bishop Scory of Hereford. Rowberry Street is the "back street" both to the "new street" (High Street and Broad Street) and to the old church property and the original street, Church Street. The street was probably in existence by the first town survey of 1285 but wasn't available for burgage holdings until 1356 when the bishop gave up occupation of the manor as part of the retrenchment which followed the Black Death.

The little stone building which is now Terry Smith's garage was where the fire engine was kept in the 19th century. Between that and the vicarage lands there developed a piece called "Barley Close", still the name of three houses.

Schallenge Walk is a modern development, but the name comes from a rare dialect word meaning "lychgate", the entrance to the churchyard. Schallenge House, tucked in on the footpath which runs to the churchyard, is the former Cottage Hospital, rebuilt, as an inscription on the front records, in time for Queen Victoria's Golden Jubilee in 1887. Its predecessor of 1869 had been the converted old Toll House (not a turnpike cottage, but the house where market tolls were levied), which had become too small for a hospital.

That house had come to be known as the Deanery, dating from the time between 1822 and 1833 when the vicar was Charles Scott Luxmoore also Rector of Cradley and Dean of St. Asaph. A crusading pamphlet of 1835 reckoned that his income in the St. Asaph diocese was £3,006, and that his total church income was £6,356. He was not in Bromyard very often - during these twelve years there were 380 baptisms in Bromyard - Luxmoore conducted 33 of them; 181 marriages - Luxmoore officiated at 17; and there were 570 burials, of which Luxmoore performed 33. In 1829 he managed just one of these occasional offices and in 1830 none. When he was in Bromyard he lived not in the new vicarage built by Dr. Cope only ten or twenty years before, but in "Church House". For years after it was known as the "Old Deanery".

There was a great debate in 1887 about whether to move the hospital to another site, because of the smell from the churchyard – it contained an enormous cesspool, and was used for "gruntage" by the townsmen (a word I can't trace, but it must have meant dumping rubbish). The vicar, Mr. Martin, thought the smell would die away, and the existing building, now a private house, was erected.

With the deaths of Mr. Martin and of Henry Barneby of Bredenbury the support for the hospital waned, and in the early years of the 20th century it had few patients and was often in debt. In 1913 there was a public meeting to consider closing the hospital owing to lack of funds and debt. It was pointed out that it had been established in 1869 when there was no railway or other means of getting to Worcester or Hereford. In 1918 it was decided to close the hospital: the finances were inadequate and there had been only 13 patients last year. Gradually the Linton Workhouse on the Worcester Road assumed more of the character of a local hospital.

On the site of the recently built Merchants Court there seems to have been a farmyard as late as 1850 when Benjamin Herschel Babbage reported to the General Board of Health on "the Sewerage, Drainage, Supply of Water, and the Sanitary Condition of the Inhabitants of the Town of Bromyard." He wrote, among other expressions of disgust at the unhealthy state of the town, "The south side of [Back-Street] consists almost entirely of stables and other back premises belonging to High Street and Broad Street. An open drain runs along this side of the street and receives the drainage from these premises together with that from a slaughterhouse and one whole side is literally studded with manure heaps. In this street I found a farmyard, it being on the outskirts of the town, the whole of which was reeking with a large amount of dung, straw and filth, in the process of decomposition, whilst in the centre stood a pump surrounded by stagnant water upon every side." There is nowhere in the road where this could have been but the site of Merchants Court. It is perfectly possible that at some stage in the 17th and/or 18th centuries the timber-framed house next door had been a farm house with an adjacent yard, that it had ceased to be such when farmers preferred to live outside towns, and that the farm *yard* had continued for decades in Back Street.

Much later there was on the site a warehouse/outlet for Mayne's the ironmongers in Market Square. Peter Gilbert says it was a sort of Nissen hut.

NEWS & RECORD PRINT SHOP EARLY 20TH C.

The timber-framed house opposite Peter Gilbert's yard, whose style is said by Tonkin to be that of a farmhouse, was built around 1600 on the site of an earlier hall house. It is not a particularly grand building, and not in a good position – in the middle of the 17th century the pig market was held in the street! The back of the brick extensions to its east end is an old malthouse. The present name of the west portion, the Old Record House, comes from the use of that end for printing and publishing the *Bromyard News & Record* until 1955. The property was bought in 1884 by Joseph B. Weeks, maltster and corn dealer. He installed his son Vincent there in 1897 to run the newspaper.

From the later 18th century when the house was owned by the Philpott family it was let out as three dwellings. After the newspaper moved the Hunt family ran various businesses in the building.

Opposite, the street frontage of Gilbert's was a saddler. Pumphreys department store, on the High Street where the Co-op and adjoining shops are now, ran through to Rowberry Street – a very small part of their furniture showroom frontage still stands. It had brick dressings in a low arch over a door, and to right the wall has recently been rebuilt in Forest Stone. The big brick building next to Gilbert's yard was erected in 1906 as Pettifer's Garage, being at the back of their showroom on Broad Street. It replaced their earlier building, destroyed by fire.

Later it was the Milore Glove Factory (the last manager, Peter Garrett, still owns it). The Worcester based factory came to Bromyard in 1946, first setting up shop in premises at the top of Sherford Street. The factory moved several times, into Rowberry Street and then to a purpose-built factory at no. 22 Old Road – later home to a children's nursery, now redeveloped.

THE STAFF OF THE GLOVE FACTORY

Next to that is the alley that leads to Tinton's joinery, a family run firm established in 1984. A small brick building next to their dust extractors in the alleyway was Pettifer's gunpowder store, where they used to fill their own shotgun cartridges.

On the private car park next to Rowberry House stood for about twenty years from the 1940s, the garage of Burnham's Coaches. who had depots in Clifton-on-Teme and Worcester and did many of the early school runs when children had to come in to Bromyard for secondary education after 1944.

In the later 20th and 21st centuries most of the premises at the back of the burgage lots of Broad Street and High Street, stables or outhouses or workshops, have gradually been transformed into dwellings: flats or houses. The lots taper towards Rowberry Street, so these premises have shorter frontages than the shop fronts.

The Public Hall has come to rest on the third site it has had; the present building is recognisable as late 20th century by the extensive use of stone "jumpers", large stones mortared in on their edges as part of stone cladding to a block-built structure.

4. MARKET SQUARE

A market place was an essential for a medieval town. By around 1285 26 individuals had 47½ *selde* or stalls in the one here, which was larger than today's Market Square. It perhaps stretched west to the passage that runs past Tinton's joinery, and south to the rear of Flowerdew's. By 1575 it seems to have been approaching its present size, with normal burgage plots (but not apparently shops) replacing the booths. There was a High Cross there and hiring fairs for servants were held, certainly from the late 18th century.

At some point a Market House was erected (with stocks for miscreants beside it). This was pulled down in 1844 and replaced (by the vicar, who had bought the right to collect market tolls!) with a larger but unsuccessful one on the corner of Back Street and

BROMYARD MARKET HOUSE 1840 / 1842

Church Street. It was an open wooden structure with a room in the eaves. It may have been a little larger than the surviving picture of it suggests, but it was nothing like Ledbury's grand and still surviving structure. It was more like the early 16th century one surviving in Pembridge, also (this being Herefordshire) in wood. If it were still there, such activity as Morris dancing at the Folk Festival, or the meet of hounds on Boxing Day would not be so practical!

The present very attractive Market Square (attractive when it's not being used as a car park) has buildings from the 16th to the 19th centuries, many of them timber framed. The oldest is nos. 4-6, Flowerdew's, a timber framed building which originally stood forward of any other buildings. The top storey is later, and the balcony modern. The *risqué* Millennium Clock on the balcony, designed by Michael Oxenham and made by Robert Race, gave a lot of pleasure, but sadly the figures need rebuilding and have been removed.

In the 1920s the printer Alfred Walter Thursby moved the Oakley Press to these premises which he had bought and which H. E. Oakley had operated from a house in Twyning Street (or on that side of the square). The top storeys then were rendered.

To the east of Flowerdew's is a pair of timber framed buildings, built together probably in the 17th century. The timber framing was covered with stucco until the 1930s, and is exposed in the salon of Hair House. The stone building next, two storeys to the Square and three to Sherford Street, is possibly as late as the late 18th century. It was known as the Old Bakery, and was Frank Williams' confectionery as late as 1940 (see photo opposite). The oven in the kitchen is still there beyond the Sci-fi museum.

FRANK WILLIAMS IN FRONT OF HIS CONFECTIONERY

Across the road used to stand no. 12 The Square, for long Perkins' shoe and boot shop, but this was pulled down in 1938 to help traffic turning into the Square. The stone wall then built onto no. 14 (another 17th century timber framed building) is of much better quality local sandstone than most stone used in the town, full of pebbles of various sizes. The stone is said to have come from the recently demolished gaol in Hereford. Nos. 16 and 18 too are timber framed under their present stucco. There may not have been buildings here earlier than this 17th century row.

SOUTH EAST CORNER OF MARKET SQUARE BEFORE PERKINS' BOOT SHOP WAS PULLED DOWN

The Hop Pole dominates the north side, an 18th century brick building that seems to have been built on a hitherto empty site. It was much used in the 19th and early 20th century for town events and meetings, auctions, ancient survivals such as the Court Baron in 1834 and the Lord of the Manor Court in 1909, the Loyal Broxash Lodge of the Oddfellows in 1925, and even a meeting of the fledgling Local History Society in 1969. In August 1933 a case of sea lions, whose transport had broken down, stayed there, "making the night hideous with their noises." No. 11, to the right of the inn, was probably built on to it in the first half of the 19th century to provide extra staff and service accommodation. It later became a shop, and as a result of the wide trading window the upper floors are supported on cast-iron pillars.

The west side of the square and Twyning Street are 18th or early 19th centuries. Nos. 3, 5 and 7 are timber framed, of different dates, but united by a 19th century brick front. Nos. 1 and 3 Twyning Street have unusually good door cases for such a modest terrace. They probably replaced an earlier inn, the Nag's Head. No 1, The Square, on the corner with Broad Street, has its upper storeys set back. It's a 17th century timber framed building, refaced with brick in the 18th century, and raised in height and remodelled just before 1900. The shop front from then is quite sophisticated, with a moulded cornice which has consoles (brackets) with acanthus leaves on.

The last house in Market Square is no. 2, the Old Post Office, with its handsome if slightly wonky 18th century brick front, and off-centre doorway. It has many fine interior features, including the original post office counter. The two bay windows are quite different, the one on the right being especially attractive – though difficult to repair when a lorry recently rolled off the parking area into it!

How have things changed in 175 years? In 1841 the heads of households in Market Square were a surveyor (living at the Hop Pole), an auctioneer, an attorney's clerk, a shoemaker, a corn dealer, a grocer, a plumber, a butcher, a cabinet maker, a glover, a stationer, a baker, a grocer, a chemist and druggist, a solicitor, and a lady who was described as "independent" (of independent means). Maybe there are not so many people living over their businesses now, but there's still a butcher, a carpet shop, a couple who have just retired as a clock mender and furniture restorer, also having an antiques business, another antique shop also a workshop, an artist's studio (until recently a wool shop), two cafés, a museum, an accountant, a hairdresser, the Hop Pole, and what might have surprised the early Victorians, a charity shop. But change has been constant: in 1851 all but four heads of households were different, and changes went on each census. Some folk went up in the world: William Wall, "lath-cleaver" in 1861, was "timber merchant" in 1871.

5. BROAD STREET

Broad Street, you will hardly need telling, is part of the *vicus novus* which had been added to Bishop Capella's 1120s town by the 1270s. At times the name has been used for the whole road up to Cruxwell Street, but I'm just writing now about the present Broad Street up to Pump Street.

When we looked at the Market square we noticed that this originally stretched a little further west than the present frontage; the old line can be seen inside the property which is 5 Twyning Street and 42 Rowberry Street, now being excellently renovated as one dwelling. An even older boundary of the square may be the strange crooked alley which runs past Tinton's joinery through to Rowberry Street.

In this alley part of Tinton's was an early workshop for Morgan cars, an enterprise of the son of the vicar of Stoke Lacy, Prebendary Morgan, who financed much of the firm's development and ran its financial affairs for years.

In the later days of street markets the butter and poultry markets were in Broad Street with farm wives on the pavement outside the Falcon and a market room in the inn for dairy produce and dressed poultry. In 1890 J. B. Weeks recalled buying live poultry opposite the Falcon around 1860. Eventually this market moved to the King's Arms yard. He was the corn chandler and maltster in Broad Street (who doubled as Clerk to The Highway Board, to Bromyard Charity Trustees, & to The Commissioners of Land & Assessed Taxes, and bought the timber framed house in Rowberry Street so that his son could run the *Bromyard Record* in the western end).

Two late 17th century ventures were in Broad Street. One was the school founded by the will of the Revd. Phineas Jackson in 1681; that was on the corner of Frog Lane and will be dealt with under that street. Then there were the Quakers who had had a meeting house in the High Street from 1677 and who built a new one behind 16 Broad

Street in 1726. The number of Friends declined in the 18th century, partly because of fines for failing to pay demands for tithes to support the vicar. At the religious census of 31 March 1851 only four Friends attended. The meetings revived after Henry Pumphrey and his colleague Charles Binyon came to the town in the early 20th century, but after Binyon's death in 1937 the Meeting House was closed and then sold in 1939. It had been used by the Salvation Army, by Guides and Cubs, and intermittently by the various primary schools when they needed extra premises. Sadly it was demolished about 1976. The burial ground was disused by 1850 when Babbage, in the report into the town's sanitary condition mentioned under Rowberry Street, said that it was being used as "a cattle yard, which was in a very filthy state." It was excavated by Archenfield Archaeology in 2002-3, and as with the Chapel in

FRIENDS MEETING HOUSE BEFORE DEMOLITION

Sherford Street careful excavation produced a very full report. Fifteen graves were examined, mostly showing evidence for coffins which were not always used by the austere Quakers. Features associated with the 19th Century tannery were also exposed by the ground works: wooden dye pits, a brick lined oval pit and walls of former tannery buildings.

One of the most striking buildings in Broad Street is Lloyds Bank, notable for the Portland Stone dressings which as so often with banks are meant to stand for commercial security. It is full of fossils, of which oyster shells are the easiest to recognise. It was built in 1886-7 as the Old Worcester Bank, the architects being Yeates and Jones of Worcester. That bank lasted from 1781 to 1906 before amalgamating. Many people will remember that in 2011 it suffered an attempt to break in with a JCB and remove the ATM... you can still see the repaired brickwork.

Most of the premises in Broad Street have a long history of use as different shops, inns, private houses; the Local History Society is beginning to compile a history of the different use of each shop in both Broad and High Streets. For instance, the premises opposite Pump Street, no. 1 Broad Street, with an early 19th century front and modern shop front, has been an eating place under various names since 1977. In the early 20th century it was a draper's, Fanny Hobday in 1911, then Feltham's, in 1941 J S Foot. In 1950 it was Woods Windows and also sold motor bikes; in 1960 it was Wallis furniture. It is one of the brick-fronted buildings which is actually a timber-framed structure, here of 1616 with an interesting staircase. The whole of the burgage plot has been filled with undistinguished ancillary buildings, which gives the present Fox and Badger a surprisingly large dining area.

The new sewing and haberdashery shop was briefly the Tourist Information Centre, before that Olive's Wool, earlier Arrowsmith's fruit and veg, and much earlier where Pettifer's were first.

No. 16, with a more elaborate 19th century brick façade than most – pilasters and keystones - was for most of the 20th century a boot and shoe shop – Herbert Lloyd, then Ross, then Peter Briggs. Briefly an antique shop, it was Wardrobe dress shop and is now called

Hourglass. Like many houses in the centre of the town it has a large cellar and the rear is of coursed rubble; perhaps the stone had been dug out to make the cellar. Duncan James, in the very full study of the historic buildings in the town centre which he carried out in 2008 (see Further Reading), thought the core was 18th century, unlike the handsome no. 18 next door which probably like so many others in the street has a 17th century core.

No. 30 (above) was a butcher's for years, with a slaughter house behind, now I think converted to dwellings.

Not many Bromyard shops have stuck-on plaques of showy rock, which has been a common fashion in recent years. A rare example is no. 6-8, which was Top B Frocks, and recently an antique and furniture shop, no. 8. It has some panels of a showy blue-black igneous rock from south east Norway called Larvikite. This is sometimes called "Blue Pearl Granite" by sellers of stone, but it is not a granite to a geologist. It has large silvery and bluish feldspar crystals which get their effect from "labradorescence", an optical phenomenon to do with how the crystals are arranged. It is just under 300 million years old. The panels are well set in the woodwork of an Art Deco shopfront probably put in by the Midlands Electricity Board in the late 1940s or 1950s. In 1909 the shop was "Jones" and there were also dentists in the building. The building is probably 18th century, re-fronted late in the 19th. Typically the rear of the building is coursed rubble possibly from the excavation of the cellar. The two floor apartment behind the Flemish bond bricks above the shop front now makes a commodious flat for the proprietors of the Falcon next door.

Opposite is one of the most interesting and most historic buildings in the town, the shop portion now once again licensed premises as Oaklands café. It was for a century and a half the Red Lion, then the Lion public house but closed about 1938. Whether it was built as a hostelry is uncertain, but it seems to have been re-modelled about the time it is first known of as an inn, in 1789. The upper storeys originally jettied out, but have been under-built, and the centre and right bays also added to outwards. It is an early to mid-17th century timber framed building, and like the Falcon was covered with stucco until the last century. The stucco was part of the re-modelling, along with the three sash windows. The right hand bay has moulded plaster decorations on the ceiling: seven fleur-de-lys, three roses, and a bird, haphazardly arranged.

At some stage the building came into possession of the Tomkins family who built up the Buckenhill estate over nearly a century and a half. In 1789 The Revd. Packington G. Tomkins, the last of the family at Buckenhill, sold the property to his tenant Thomas Thorne for £210, and then Thorne sold it on to Richard Weeks for £235. Weeks had an older son, also Richard, who was a saddler who joined the army at the age of 23 and spent almost all of his over 18 years service in the Mediterranean, helping keep Napoleon's troops out of Malta, the Ionian Islands, and Egypt. When he finally came back to Bromyard he was lucky to find work as a turnpike gate keeper; not all veterans were so fortunate.

By then the elder Richard in his will of 1814 had left money to mortgage the property in order to let Maria, the widow of his second son John, occupy it, the eventual beneficiaries to be his grandsons Vincent and Thomas Weeks when they came of age. Weeks had recently erected a brewery behind the main building, and the stables gave onto Back Street. The mortgage was bought out in 1828 for £300 by the widow (apparently under her maiden name of Maria Burraston) and she held the licence for some years.

In 1830, Thomas and Vincent having come of age, Thomas sold his half share to Vincent who was the licensee until his death in 1869. Various family members scratched their names on the window glass of the upstairs sitting room in 1853. Vincent left the Red Lion to his son Edward, who took on the licence, mortgaged the property in 1872, and on dying in 1876 left all to his wife. If she married again the inn was to be sold with first refusal to his brother Joseph (they had married sisters). Joseph, as we've seen, had other interests – he was superintendent registrar, besides helping with the town charities, the football club and so on - and the inn was sold to Thomas H. Lewis of Malpas, Lewis and Co. of Worcester.

He rented the Red Lion for £25 a year as a tied house to James Tarbath, a local carrier and mail cart contractor who continued that business and also became in 1906 the overseer of the workhouse. Joseph Weeks kept the tenancy of the malthouse to the rear. When Tarbath died just before the First World War his wife Agnes took over the licence and held it till her death at 91 – reputedly the oldest licensee in Britain. The Brewster Sessions then refused to re-licence the pub – there were quite enough in Bromyard. During the war, the old Red Lion was Westminster School's library while the school was based in Buckenhill, and after the war one of the masters, Mr. Claridge, remained in Bromyard and kept the bookshop going for the general public. After him, it was run for some years by Mr.B.C Howe. In the early 1980s it was the offices of the Citizens Advice Bureau and then of Age Concern; later it was a children's shop and then a gift shop. Following new 21st century needs of the public it was recently a computer shop, which also dealt in the 19th century new technology of bicycles.

THE WESTMINSTER SCHOOL BOOK SHOP, NOW OAKLANDS CAFE

Either side of this historic house are interesting pairs of buildings. To the right are the two shops in which Peter Gilbert and his father before him have built up, first in the right half of the pair, a remarkable range of businesses: fish and chips, fruit and veg, household goods, hardware, everything for your horse. Only the first of these provinces of the empire has been let go. A Bromyard institution!

To the left no. 3 Broad Street is a particularly fine 18th century brick fronted town house, now apartments after a period as a solicitor's and then an antique shop. The rear elevation is the poor quality coursed rubble stone so typical of Bromyard's hidden sides. The further and larger of two ranges behind has escaped the original burgage plot and now lies back from Rowberry Street.

6. FROG LANE

With Frog Lane we're back to one of the early streets – probably the *vicus de meydenswelle* in the *Red Book* of 1285, which lists 19 burgage holders there sharing 12½ burgages, paying twelve pence a burgage. They included some people from the surrounding area: Johnes de Colewalle, Bronnyng de Ffrom, Rogus de Monderfeld, Matild de Lynton, and from further afield: Emma de Stodleye and Nichus de Stoodleye. There was a mercer, two "taylours", and "Molend", probably a miller. Surnames were just forming; Wittms Talp (or his father) must have made people think of a mole!

The street would have run right through to Linton Lane, as indeed it did until the bypass was built, and may originally have had a much wider entry from Broad Street before the charity school founded under the will of the vicar, The Revd. Phineas Jackson, in 1681. This was to be run by a "school-dame" who would teach "poor children to read, knit, and sew plain work when they were fit and of capacity to learn,… mean children whose parents are really poor." In the early 19th century it was "in a very ruinous state" and there had been no teaching there since the "old woman" who kept it fell ill and died. In 1825 the Bromyard Charity Trustees decided to close the school, exchange the site for one the vicar made available in his kitchen garden, and unite with the efforts of the newly formed National Society (for Promoting the Education of the Poor in the Principles of the Established Church in England and Wales). The old school building was a plumber's in 1911, a butcher's in the 1940s – London Central Meat, then Canterbury Meat; then for some years it was a greengrocer's, Neil Davidson 1976-9, then Alan Gilbert; then it was House Mistress furnishing, then Escape, a beauty shop. The building is now a shop, the one storey, isolated, 22 Broad Street, recently successively a candle shop, a hair salon and now a monumental mason's. The front has been rebuilt, but the massive pillars of the blocked side door are still there.

Why the road became Frog Lane is not known; Maidwell Lane was still an alternative as late as 1776. That is in the later of two lots of 18th century deeds which survive in the Local History Centre archives showing that there were orchards, one portion converted to a hop yard, where Bishop's Garage is now. In 1711 one orchard belonged to Mrs. Mary Barneby, widow of John, the fourth Barneby of Brockhampton, another adjacent to it to Richard Davies, barber. This land was originally the grounds of Sherford House, which stretched across where the bypass is now. An orchard where apple trees were bred survived on part of the land until the 1960s.

Hat House preserves the memory and probably some of the masonry of a three storey 19th century house hatter's shop making green top hats. Above and behind it the slaughterhouse is now a dwelling, but still keeping its name. At the southern end from 1913 to 1957 was St. Joseph's church, designed and built by the redoubtable Belgian Father Denys Matthieu as the first RC church in the town. Its address was sometimes given as Bishall Walk, after Bishall House the far side of Linton Lane. In 1923 Fr Denys built a small parish hall, and in 1932 he was not allowed to use two railway carriages in an orchard there as dwelling houses.

FR. DENYS MATHIEU

In the 1920s the town Fire Engine House moved there from Rowberry Street and remained until 1937. Its door to the lane is still there, behind which is now a new shed for the last house in the Tanyard, and on that western side were also at one time tennis courts.

THE OLD FIRE ENGINE SHED DOOR

Tanhouse Terrace dates from the 1930s; the gardens are at an angle to the houses, so the bottom one (whose garage is the remains of stables for the horses of J. W. Williams, the main town grocer) has the longest length.

Beyond its end, also now in The Tanyard, was a corn dryer (with access from Pump Street), later taken over by Baywood Chemicals who had a branch in the 1960s in Sherford House.

Somewhere in the lane were at various times other activities: in 1926 a warehouse owned and used by Pearson Davies (possibly the one later owned by the Urban District Council burnt down in 1950), from 1929 for some years a branch of the Shropshire, Worcestershire, and

Staffordshire Electric Power Company, and in the late 1930s and 1940s an infants' school.

Where the new houses at the top stand were the garages of Weale and Batemans, the bakers in Broad Street.

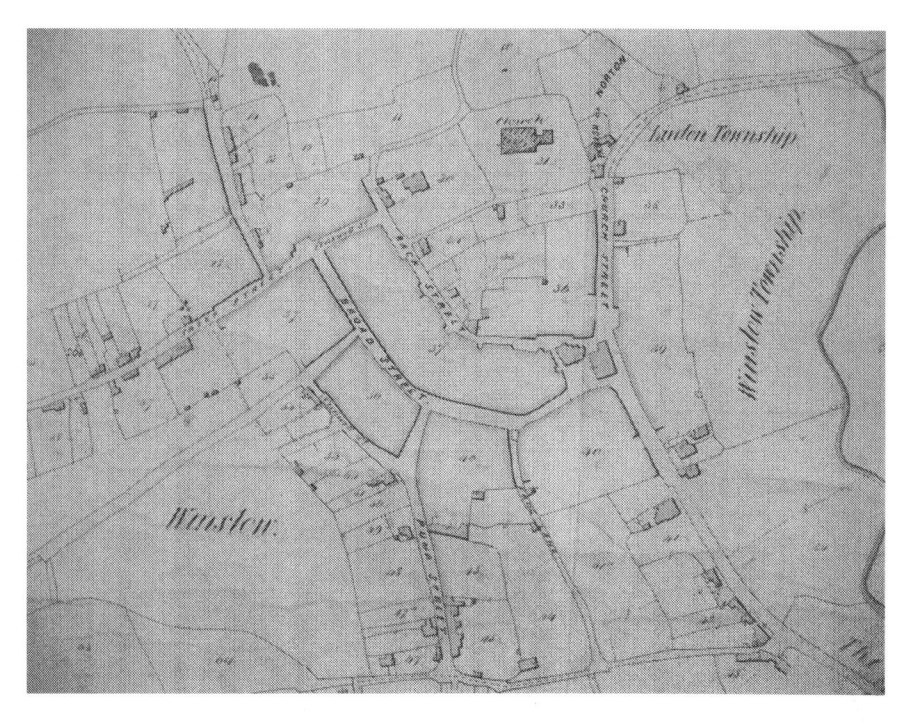

TITHE MAP 1844

7. PUMP STREET AND TOWER HILL

Like so many streets in the town, Pump Street has had other names. In the survey of about 1285 the first section is unnamed and has no burgage plots, being just an opening between two of the plots in *vicus novus* (High Street). It then joins *vicus de stonhulle*, Little Hereford Street, in which 32 men and 5 women held, most of them, half a burgage plot each. This road ran up to join Linton Lane, presumably at the "stone hill" (no ancient quarry can now be identified in the area). By 1575 and the next survey the name had changed to Nunwalle Streate. The name is a puzzle, as there is no record of any nunnery in Bromyard. Nor is it known why a late 17th century house in the street should be called "Nunwell *Priory*" when there had never been a priory there!

By 1788 another name was coming in; George Badham, a soap boiler, agreed with the churchwardens and the overseers of the poor (all the local government there was) to put in for a guinea and keep in repair for twenty years (at 7s. 6d. a year) a pump belonging to the town "erected and placed in a certain well there called Nunwell being in Nunwell Street otherwise the Pump Street." Where exactly was this pump? It's not on the large scale OS map of 1887.

37

Tower Hill was part of Pump Street until the by-pass was built. Tower House is one of the largest, finest, and also one of the latest timber-framed house in Bromyard, dating from about 1630. It's an old tradition that Charles I spent the night of 3 September 1643 there with the well-connected Mrs. Baynham. As with the Falcon, a Georgian façade was removed in the early 20th century to reveal the fine timber framing.

In Pump Street was an important commercial enterprise, the tannery, which lasted into the 20th century, probably closing before 1914. It had extensive buildings, tanning pits, and a very tall chimney to

TANYARD STAFF, LATE 19TH CENTURY

carry away the unpleasant smells. The tanner's Tan House is late 18th century, with a fine pedimented doorway flanked by windows also with pediments, and with large shutters.

Nunwell House opposite is on the site of an 18th century inn, the Seven Stars. It was built around 1800, in smallish bricks laid in Flemish bond, with a hipped roof. The bay windows are later. Its grounds, described when the house was sold in 1886 as "ornamental park-like meadow", stretched across where the by-pass came to Tower Hill Terrace. It was the doctor's residence and surgery until 1961. In the Local History Centre is a nurseryman's bill showing that the great Wellingtonia was planted about 1910. When the new surgery was built in the grounds, it was for several years a spring factory. After it stopped being the factory Nunwell House was divided vertically, front and back now being separate dwellings.

The Falcon Mews opposite was originally stables, then a garage, and in 1947 became the town cinema for some years.

Now conspicuously on the corner with the by-pass is the former Primitive Methodist chapel of 1899, designed by A. Hill Parker of Worcester, who also designed Brockhampton School. The new *Buildings of England – Herefordshire* thinks it may just qualify as the only example in the county of "Free Perp", "much favoured by Nonconformists elsewhere in England"; James Tonkin in *Bromyard: A Local History* says "that it shows how far the late-Victorian builders had strayed from the architectural rules of their predecessors." It did not last long as a chapel; it was taken over by the Local Education Authority after Methodist reunification in 1932 centralised their worship at the Wesleyan Chapel in New Road. It was at first used as a technical training workshop. It was then used to print the *Bromyard News and Record* in the 1950s, with the premises of Handley and James, undertakers, below, and is now a number of dwellings.

8. HIGH STREET

It's taken a long time to reach the High Street, which readers will not need telling is part of the *vicus novus*, the new street added to the town sometime in the late 12th or early 13th century when it was clear that Bishop de Capella's experiment of a new town on his manor was a success. Originally it was lined with burgage plots, long thin parcels of land which on the east side ran right through to Back Street (now Rowberry Street) and on the west side to the original edge of the town.

All the houses are basically at right angles to the street, with the burgage plot running behind, usually measuring originally some 180-190 feet. The original burgage frontages are hard to estimate because of divisions and amalgamations, but seem to have been mostly, according to Phyllis Williams' calculations, 41 feet. Some, again, like nos. 34-6, have rubble stone rear walls.

The earliest known occupiers of properties in *vicus novus*, New Street, in 1275 or so, included two tailors, Emma and Peter, a dealer in fish, Milo, a chaplain, Nicholas, a miller, Walter, and three "marshals", Peter, Stephen, and William. As early as this document, and in small settlements, "marshal" mainly meant a farrier or horse-doctor, though it was beginning also to mean a law officer, especially one responsible for keeping order and looking after prisoners. People originating in neighbouring villages included Reginald from Munderfield, Agnes from Grendon, William from Wacton, Matilda from Evesbatch, Walter from Frome, Hugh from Stoke (Lacy?)

I'm starting at the top on the left or west side, because on the corner with Cruxwell Street is what currently appears to be the oldest surviving building in the town, the interior of nos. 55-59, an L-plan house probably of the mid-15th century, now hiding behind boring 19th century painted brick. It seems that in Bromyard as in most other English towns earlier humbler buildings were rebuilt in the increasing prosperity of the centuries when the country had recovered from the Black Death of the mid-14th century. Newsagents have been on the corner for at least sixty years.

The shoe shop was in the 1940s and '50s a shop Bromyard currently lacks – a gents' outfitters. The dog grooming and the pet supplies shops have both had a great variety of uses, whereas the betting shop has been that, under different names, since at least 1974. Before and after WW1 a motor engineer, Edmund Williams, had the property, and in the 1960s it was the office of Russell, Baldwin and Bright.

EDMUND WILLIAMS' GARAGE – c 1910

It's strange to remember that not so long ago the card shop and the travel agents were Legges the butcher, now in Tenbury Road. There was a previous butcher there, but before that there was a car showroom, and in the 1920s a draper.

Further down towards New Road there are a number of jettied out upper floors, including at the King's Arms. This has the feature of the larger inns of a big yard at the back which would originally have had access to Little Hereford Street. There is also at the King's Arms a fine stack of grouped chimney shafts with diagonal ribs giving a star-shaped section. Below are more timber-framed buildings with later fronts. The King's Arms was built as such.

The inn was bought by an incomer named Thomas Taylor in the 1740s; after his death it was run for many years by his second wife Joyce Daykin whom he married at Stanford Bishop. They had sons Thomas, currier in Eardisland who married Ann Philpotts (their children inherited a significant estate from Ann's uncle); James, apothecary of Birmingham; Joseph, schoolmaster of Kempsey; and Henry, saddler of Bromyard; and daughters Althea, wife of Francis Bengham, hop merchant of Bridgnorth; and Mary, whose husband Philip Bray, later became licensee of the King's Arms.

The yard of the inn was the final home of the last two of the Bromyard elephants, the remnants of the circus brought by Ada Chapman at the beginning of the Second World War first to Suckley and then to Tack Farm. By the winter of 1942-3 the surviving two were in an outhouse at the back of the King's Arms. A Westminster School pupil, Frank Herrman, was ill that winter and so not with the rest of the evacuated school at Buckenhill or one of the other local properties used by the school, but with his mother, a part-time teacher at the school. She lodged at the King's Arms, and Frank's room overlooked the yard "where there was constant to-ing and fro-ing as the elephants were taken out for exercise once or even twice a day. But, for reasons I never discovered, there was insufficient fodder for the elephants during the winter."

"So, first one, then a second died. All efforts, even with tractors, to remove them from the brewhouse failed. I frequently watched this out of my small sickroom window. In the end, a butcher was called to cut up the huge carcasses so that they could be dragged out in sections. It was a most grisly business and took several days."

"I watched, spellbound and horrified, as the tractors eventually hauled out the sections with enormous clanking chains. The exhaust fumes as the engines strained were overpowering, as in those days tractors used a mix of paraffin and low-grade petrol as fuel."

The butcher who cut them up was Jack Rimell, whose shop was in the High Street near the King's Arms. It was presumably these elephants which were buried near Broad Bridge.

The corner with New Road, now Rowland's, has been a chemists' since at least the 1890s.

Across the road nos. 58-62 has a substantial 17th century house behind its dull 20th century brick front. The corner premises, now Caleb Roberts insurance brokers, have been "white collar" since at least the 1980s, but a century ago were a baker's and corn merchant, in the Mason family for two generations.

No. 54, a private house, has a long rear 16-17th century wing. Lamings have been in their premises, baking bread, since 1959, and there has been a baker there at least since 1911. In the 19th century the baker and his family lived over the shop. The new funeral shop and the new(-ish) florists' have both had a great variety of uses. The Steak bar has been an eatery since 1941; in the early 1960s it was the Bluebell café run by a couple called Hinckesman (nothing to do with the local family spelt slightly differently.)

The former NatWest bank (formerly the National Provincial) is early 19th century with the typical imposing entrance to show the bank's probity. In 1876 its hours were 10-3, but it stayed open an extra hour on Mondays and Fair days. Nos. 34-6 have the typical rough stonework at the rear with neat late 18th century fronts which we have seen to be so typical of Bromyard buildings. No. 32 is an early 19th century remodelling of an 18th century house; dental patients today know that it has fine plasterwork mouldings and a handsome (if hazardous) staircase. It has been a dental practice since at least the 1950s; previously doctors were living and practising there.

The Queen's Arms inn is basically late 16th century, although the front was rebuilt in the late 19th; it was originally the Leopard, and old-fashioned people still call the useful passage through to Rowberry Street "the Leopard entry". The name was changed, patriotically, to the Wellington Arms in 1822, and then, presumably with a political change of landlord, to the Grey Arms in 1835. It had settled down to the neutral Queen's Arms by 1851.

All this upper part of High Street was the beast market until the late 19th century and the establishment of the Smithfield in Milvern Lane (Tenbury Road).

The Bay Horse, now rather regrettably The Inn at Bromyard, was once two adjoining inns. The small square panelling of the left façade is unusual, and inside is a ceiling with moulded ribs and frieze alternating *fleurs-de-lys* and roses. The right hand façade was raised in the 18th century and is close-studded (adjoining vertical planks of wood). Nos. 23-27 seem late 18th century, with their two plain brick fronts, but have three gables to the rear, suggesting another substantial timber-framed house, perhaps late 16th century.

The former HSBC Bank on the corner of Pump Street was built for the Midland Bank in 1922 and is typical of the style of single storey pavilions with classical detail which that bank put up in many towns (compare the one in Brecon). Brick with stone dressings is common; the stone here is a beach deposit, sandy with shells. With on-line banking and other changes banks are deserting small towns and this striking building is now apartments.

FORMER HSBC BANK

Next door, Gladwin's, brick with half-timbered gables, is about 1900.

On the opposite side, High Street begins with a mid-19th century block with moulded windows, and some of the following brick fronts have timber-framed cores.

Flavours has been an Indian restaurant for ten or more years. Earlier it had been Burton's grocers, managed between the wars by Dick Royall, whose father had been the licensee of the Rose and Lion, and who had joined up in World War 1 at the age of 15.

PUMPHREYS

The Co-op was the left hand end of the enormous Pumphreys department store which lasted for most of the 20th century and ran right through to Rowberry Street; before becoming the Co-op it was other multiple grocers: Spar, Alldays.

The barber's shop, Food For All, and the shop in between, have all had very varied businesses over the years. Lin's Wok, the Chinese takeaway, has been the home of various eateries for forty or more years.

J.W.WILLIAMS & SONS, GROCERS

Johnson's showroom was from about 1845 to about 1970 the large grocer's J. W. Williams, who also had a depot at the station. After they closed it became the International Stores, then a Spar shop, then Poundland, and then was empty for a while, so there were rejoicings when Johnson's fitted out such a prominent site.

It may seem curious that this showroom is rarely open, and that customers are directed to the other showroom in Church Street; but probably the attraction to Johnson's is the yard at the back opening onto Rowberry Street, where all their vehicles can be parked.

9. NEW ROAD

So far we've looked at some of the old streets of the medieval town and seen what's become of them. Now we turn to the street which marked the first big change to the pattern. Before 1835 getting out of the town towards Hereford was rather odd; you had to go to (Little) Hereford Street (sometimes Back Lane), which went through to Old Road, and then turn past the still existing row of brick and stone cottages (which had a blacksmith's shop and are 17th century with a 19th century façade). You then had to go through Holditch Gate and up Piccadilly Hill to the Piccadilly toll house where the turnpike road, the present main road from Hereford, joins the A44. There is still a house called Piccadilly at the beginning of Hereford Road (although it's quite a recent building), and one called Old Ditch Cottage off Little Hereford Street. Beyond Old Ditch Cottage a fence now bars the way where the gate was; you can easily imagine a road climbing the hill ahead, but all traces had gone by the time of the 1886 Ordnance Survey 1/2500 map.

In 1835 a fine new Hereford road was cut through, right to High Street, necessitating the removal of part of the building now Rowland's and, eventually, the attractive remodelling of what is now Bufton's. Much of it was edged with stone walls, the typical lowish Bromyard walls of local sandstone with massive coping stones, some beautifully dressed to cubic triangles; a lot of these walls have gone but there are some good ones near the bottom of the road.

The road, after an initial shallower portion, is on an even gradient of 1:11. (The usual recommended gradient for horse-drawn vehicles was 1:30!) The hillside was rather steep half way up, so this meant constructing a raised causeway – later houses and gardens nestle below it in an unusual fashion. This new road ran to the Piccadilly turnpike on the Hereford road and then bent to the right in order to run up to the Mount toll house at the beginning of the Leominster turnpike road, hitherto reached chiefly up Old Road, though the 1831-3 OS map shows that a lane also came up from just beyond the

Piccadilly turnpike to Flaggoners Green. This portion of New Road is now of course called West Hill.

So this new pattern of roads is what appears on the tithe maps of Bromyard and Winslow of 1844. There were a few cottages in the Piccadilly area, but the houses came gradually, as the 1886 map shows. The Rose and Lion was an early building, there at least by 1851.

ROSE AND LION, LATE 19TH C.

Nos. 8-18 are early too; nos. 12-14 with original porches, nos. 16-18 still in the rather old-fashioned Flemish bond style of brickwork, with elliptical-headed windows.

The early pair of no. 37, Croft Villa, and no. 39 still exist, with Flemish bond brickwork and handsome, rather severe, wooden porches, the two houses curiously stepped because of the gradient. Mount Pleasant, nos. 54 and 56, are also on the 1886 map, quite plain, with rendered façades, dormers, and like nos. 37-39 having a curious wavy soffit under the guttering. Next up, on the northern side, nos. 58-60 are also pre-1886; they have intriguing low iron work railings to the bedroom windows – surely not nearly high enough to stop a determined child falling out? – and rather graceful barge boards.

This grander style reached its apogee in 1906-8 with the building by Newbold (who lived in The Lilacs opposite) of nos.44-46 and 48-50. These were damned by James Tonkin in *Bromyard – A Local History*: "homes of presumably some of the business and professional Bromyard men. Of red brick with all varieties of stone mouldings and lots of unnecessary, fussy detail." Taste has changed since 1970; what detail is necessary and what unnecessary? They use terracotta, including for the tops of the gate pillars and along the top of the roadside walls. The terracotta tops of the pillars of no. 48 were smashed by vandals and replaced in Forest of Dean gritstone, which was used also to replace the bay window – the original stone looks like oolitic limestone, "Bath" stone.

The large nos. 66-68, Cranford and Claremont, nos. 72-74 and what are now called nos. 20-26 West Hill are going down the same stylistic route: finials, crockets and what not, but not yet so far. No. 72 has what looks like its original wicket gate out to the road. Nos. 5-15 West Hill appear to be humbler late Victorian semis. No. 50 (now called Kirk Brae, but Selborne up to 1967) was at one point owned by the Binyons and let to the church for use as the curate's house – rather grand for such a humble minister. It is interesting that the "business and professional men" of that period, with their hordes of children and servants, opted for semi-detached not detached houses – a trend across the country.

Lower down, no. 36 below the road and set back behind its attractive garden, is a pretty *cottage orné* near the police station. This is on the site of the Picturedrome opened in May 1914 "in the fashionable quarter of Bromyard" *with electric lighting*, temporarily closed in 1921 "because of shortage of gas", renamed in the 1930s the Plaza

Talkie Theatre and closed by 1945. Below is a terrace of four houses end on to the street and below it; a saw mill is marked here on the 1928 edition of the 25" OS map. Then comes the brick Wesleyan Methodist chapel of 1857 by Pearson & Son of Ross-on-Wye. This was originally rather severe but received an elaborate Perpendicular style porch in 1911; its oolitic stone dressings have calcite veins where some of the oolites, millennia ago, underwent pressure solution and re-crystallized.

OPENING OF PORCH, WESLEYAN CHAPEL, 1911

Gradually there was infilling; Kerioth House, now gone, was built in the 1920s when access to a surfaced road was an asset and a position on a main road still had status rather than the disadvantages of too much traffic.

One of the most recent developments, Buttsfield House run by Festival Housing, is a distinguished modern variety on the terrace.

You have to be 60 to live there, and you get with your 1 bedroom apartment a community alarm service, lounge, laundry, and guest facilities. It recalls an alternative name used in the 1760s for Prestley Field, one of the great common fields of early Bromyard which lay south of the old Hereford road. Probably it was then the site of the butts where shooting was practised.

William Madders, born about 1860, son of a carpenter at Flaggoners Green where there was a 'spital tree' factory for spade or fork handles, was later a grocer in Ledbury. He remembered that "There used to be a brickyard where the School Cookery Canteen later stood. I well remember seeing children running with the wet clay in wooden moulds from the brickmaker and placing them in long moulds to dry in the sun preparatory to their being burnt in the kilns." He also noted that there had been a clothing factory in New Road which employed twenty 'hands' which was on the site of the garage at the bottom of the road; this had been started by Donald McIntosh, draper and outfitter in the High Street who in 1885 was advertising for girls to work as machinists in the factory or at home.

DEMOLITION OF THE TOWN'S SECOND PUBLIC HALL (IN NEW ROAD)
2001

10. CRUXWELL STREET

Nowadays Cruxwell Street just stretches from Tenbury Road to Rowberry Street, but in the *Red Book* of about 1285 the *vicus de crokeswalle* must have stretched much further west, because it had well over 30 burgages, most of them held as half burgages, and two "parcells". Phyllis Williams thought it was originally "Crosswall". Later it was where the sheep market was held, and its extension west was known as Sheep Street until the 19th century. Croxewell Field was an alternative name for the 60 acre common field to the west of the town held in 40 "parcels". In the other direction, it is thought that it originally continued past the church as the Schallenge and on to the Broad Bridge and the Great Witley road. So if you like it was a small part of a significant Anglo-Saxon route linking three "minsters", monastic mission stations, Leominster, Bromyard, Kidderminster. Whether the name means the *wall* or the *well* of the cross is a moot point.

One of the oldest existing, but perhaps the most modest, of the houses in the street is the 17th century no. 6, between Annie's Anchor Café and the paper shop; it's just one bay with two rather striking sash windows, one on each floor, the upper one being inserted into timber framing with some brick infilling. It was Henry Taylor's "fruiterers" in 1911 when the two houses next door were inhabited by bootmakers and a confectioner.

In 1656 the Revd. Phineas Jackson built the stone Almshouses at the corner of what became Rowberry Street, with two-roomed accommodation for seven "poor women of good character". In the will which also provided for the school in Frog Lane, he bequeathed an income to supply the occupants of the Almshouses with beef, beer and coats. Five dwellings were occupied in 1901, one by a widow and her granddaughter; by 1911 it only housed four ladies, two widows and two spinsters. In 1954 it was under threat as "unfit for habitation", but unlike Angel House up the road, was reprieved, and in 1962 it was converted into 4 apartments. As Niklaus Pevsner points out in *Buildings of England – Herefordshire*, the doorway and the two-light window are "still entirely pre-classical".

A sad loss to Bromyard was Angel House of about 1600, which faced down the High Street and was demolished in 1957 under a "Slum Clearance Programme" energetically pursued by the Ministry of Housing and Local Government. The Medical Officer to the

ANGEL PLACE

North Herefordshire Public Health Office had condemned it too (under the Housing Act of 1936) as "unfit for habitation" in 1954 both for "disrepair" and for "sanitary defects", and although such "defects" as "lack of suitable food storage space", "lack of adequate ventilation", don't sound beyond the wit of a moderately competent architect, and although buildings in Bromyard had already received Grade II listing, no-one at that time seems to have been conscious of its value as a historic building. The Urban District Council merely discussed rehousing of the tenants (the building was owned by two partners of Bentley Hobbs & Mytton, estate agents and valuers), and by December 1956 decided it was an "eyesore" which must go. Six weeks later the *News & Record* merely commented that the new empty space "is indeed a breach in the previous cloistered look of Bromyard".

From its name, it must originally have been a hostelry. There was once a row of carved wooden figures on the front. J.G. Sanders who was born there in 1902 remembered that inside were many old oak timbers and an old oak staircase. His father's tailor's shop was downstairs; his widowed grandfather, a carpenter, lived with them in 1911. Next door was "Mrs. Maddy's house... also of old oak timber, but much larger than ours because it had two bedrooms over the archway which led to the blacksmith's house, shop and pentice, and garden plots for each house at the back, but the blacksmith's premises were not part of Angel House... Mrs. Maddy used... at General Election times to let off one or two rooms as committee rooms." (This was for the Liberal Party; their committee rooms were converted to a reading room in 1906). "In front of each house was a small flower bed and lawn with railings round them, and in front of Mrs. Maddy's house was a well with a stone trough and pump... Possibly the street name of Cruxwell may have originated from this well for I do not think there was another one in the street. There was a council mains water pump in Cruxwell Street opposite to the White Horse Inn."

The "blacksmith and implement maker" in Angel Yard, John Brace, also had an ironmonger's business in High Street, and was living there with his family, one son helping him who was an apprentice aged 13 in 1891, until 1901, when he died. Earlier the blacksmith was a relation, George Brace, and later was Henry Porter and later again John Mills, who died in 1946. Mrs Maddy, who had ten rooms in total, described herself as a boarding house keeper in 1911; she had two daughters, one a dressmaker.

Also demolished about the same time were the adjoining buildings, one which had been the doctor's practice of John Hinings when he first came to the town; later he was in the High Street and then was the first doctor in Nunwell House. In 1881, as a recent Edinburgh graduate of 26, he could afford a cook, nanny, page and groom (there were stables from which two trusses of hay were stolen that year, perhaps relying on the doctor's youth and inexperience). Probably his Yorkshire linen draper father provided finance, because he owned Nunwell House and rented it out before the son moved there. This father, who was prominent in many local affairs, ended up as a "gentleman" residing in an old manor house. Later this large Cruxwell Street building was a vet's practice, first of Samuel Chambers and then of Thomas J. Foulkes, and also the home where he had a family with not only a nanny but *three* other servants.

Cruxwell Street has always had a mixture of different classes of people living in it, with what were categorised at the time of the 1851 census as the "more substantial people" of Bromyard, for example the attorneys Philip Bray and Richard Badham, Margaret Bennet, the schoolmistress of the National School and her organist and music teacher husband John, as well as many commercial premises. There was a small Baptist church from 1859-67 next to the basket maker George Walters and opposite the toffee and rock maker Bevan. The Baptist building was later used as a warehouse. There were two tailors and a hairdresser in 1876-7, and Mrs Hannah Morley was a shopkeeper, specialising as a tripe-dresser, still there in 1891; her husband and father were carriers, an essential business up to the late 19th century when few business people had their own transport for other than local journeys.

There were in the late 19th century three taverns in Cruxwell Street, all on the north side. The White Horse on the corner of Tenbury Road was a public house in 1669 when Ann Capper, widow, made it over to her son Edward, a slaughterman. If you go round the corner you can see that there are various older portions behind the good quality red brick Georgian front in Flemish Bond, with its rather fine moulded door case. It still has by the door a ceramic plaque advertising West Country Ales, "Best in the West", although when Godfrey Devereux was licensee in 1929 he was "agent for Allsopp's Ales". Various names of licensees are known from the 19th century. Edwin Halsey was the licensee in 1875; he died and his widow ran it for a while, but by 1891 it was run as a "hotel" by a couple from Lancashire, James Park and his wife.

After he died the licensee was a widow, Mrs Mary Lewis, who had a daughter as barmaid, but in 1891 she was down the road running the Green Dragon. James's widow Jane Park was back at the White Horse with three sons helping her though only Arthur was still there in 1911, when they had a resident ostler. It closed in about 2007 and was converted into apartments.

There is a dentil cornice below the eaves on the two road-side ranges – that's bricks projecting like a row of gappy teeth. The large ground floor windows have massive limestone sills full of fossils. Just visible scratched on a brick on the corner is the broad arrow of an OS "bench mark" where the height above mean sea level was measured at the top of the town: another mark is on Petty Bridge at the bottom of the town.

THE GREEN DRAGON

The Green Dragon further east is known from about 1812 and had a brief period in the 1830s as the Unicorn. It was sold at auction in 1881 when William Price ran it as a tenant. Henry Andrews took over the licence and was still running it in 1901, a widower with three young sons; by 1911 the licensee was Charles Powis (shown above). It was demolished in the 1957 for a car park and part of the Bromyard Centre is on the site.

A different sort of tavern was no. 9, now the Therapy Centre. It was built as the temperance Coffee Tavern in 1888 for a Mr Phipp, the architect, F. W. Dorman of Northampton, giving it quite a memorable feature of first floor oriel window over two round headed windows. It was run in 1891 by Alfred Moore who lived there with his wife, small son, and a number of boarders. It was known as the Coffee Hotel in 1901 when a printer, William Barnes, lived there, and in 1911 as the Victoria Café and also the Unionist (i.e. Conservative) Club, but actually lived in by a joiner, Charles James.

As Victoria Chambers it was later the offices of Sidney Sirrell, who led a busy life as clerk to the Urban District Council, clerk to the Justices, clerk to the Local Pension Sub-Committee, clerk to the Commissioners of Taxes, correspondent to the Education Committee and clerk to the governors of the Grammar School.

It appears to have been heightened fairly recently. The row of rubble stone two storey houses beyond changed occupants frequently; and as can be seen by looking carefully, have had a complicated history of structural changes. They are now a group of apartments and for some years Peppercorn has annexed the easterly one as a garage, but were originally several different premises, most used as shops at some time.

MILK ARRIVAL IN SNOW 1947

The third Grade II listed building in the street, besides no. 6 and the former White Horse, is the large stone three storey building on the corner of Church Lane, now divided vertically (but with a flying freehold) into Peppercorn and Cruxwell House. It is 18th century, built like so much of Bromyard of rough coursed rubble stone with a tiled roof and brick chimney stacks. The east front, notes Pevsner, has a "humble pediment". The division was possible because it has a "double-depth arrangement with two hipped pitched ranges orientated north-south in line with Church Lane. They are joined with a hipped pitch at the south end." The pitched range which projects to the north was originally a dairy. There are two attractive door-cases, one on each façade, the one to Cruxwell Street being less elaborate. Almost certainly the western portion, Peppercorn, is, in fact substantially later, so it has probably absorbed two of the original two storey cottages.

11. CHURCH LANE

As part of the perimeter of the bishop's manor, Church Lane must be older than the town; and as the way to the most important mill it must have been a really significant road for centuries. Now it is a pleasant back street, and a short cut from the road along the old railway line into the town.

The first building on the right, the Tourist Information Office, is the former Heritage Centre, and was an outbuilding of the vicarage. The extension to the north is faced in a stone which doesn't otherwise appear in Bromyard: "Blue Pennant", with flecks of coal, from one of the quarries in the South Wales valleys. It is very like "Forest Stone" from the Forest of Dean, and roughly the same age, but they are different formations. The Old Vicarage was built by The Revd. Dr. George Cope around 1800, at a cost of £1,200, in local sandstone with brick dressings. It has Georgian proportions, but as James Tonkin says "the wrought-iron porch with the arched window above are Regency details". It was replaced by the present vicarage in 1965, and became the offices first of the Rural District Council and after that was abolished then of the Town Council.

On the left is, behind Cruxwell House, a former dairy range; and then the historic area of Kirkham. Both the *grim* or ducking stool and the manorial pound for stray cattle were at the entrance to this area which stretched to the Fayre Cross on the road to Tenbury, perhaps a market area before the town was founded in the 1120s. The old market significance survives in the name "Porthouse" – derived from the old Latin word *portus* which could mean a market. By the end of the 19th century a water tank on Kirkham was one of the main solutions to the long standing problems of the town's water supply. Later there were allotments on the eastern part.

There are two brick terraces on the north side; the easterly one is on the 1885 OS 25" map, marked "St. Peter's Terrace"; the westerly one, "St. Peter's Villas", nos. 5-19, appears on the 1905 revision and can be seen to have been built in two phases. The eastern four, as James Tonkin says, still have a certain Georgian look, "with a plat-band and pilasters to their brick front. Even the bricks appear to be smaller than standard and are laid in Flemish bond." The western three houses use bigger brick, and have applied timber framing on their dormer windows.

The former National School (i.e. built by the National Society for Promoting the Education of the Poor in the Principles of the Established Church in England and Wales) dates from 1862. It was designed by F. R. Kempson, the prolific Hereford-based architect and with its polychromatic brick and "Bath stone" details probably influenced the design of the Magistrates' Court and Police Station in Church Street. Known as St. Peter's, it merged in 1922 with the Nonconformist "British School" (i.e. built by the British and Foreign School Society for the Education of the Labouring and Manufacturing Classes of Society of Every Religious Persuasion) in Linton Lane. When replaced in 1989 by the new St. Peter's School in Cherry Tree Close it was well converted to housing. It was on the site of Mill Hill Court, the second of the three "portions" held by the portioners who appointed the vicars of Bromyard in the Middle Ages and down to the 19th century.

They were the joint rector of the benefice but had no other responsibility in return for the substantial income they enjoyed other than appointing a vicar (the word means substitute) to perform the spiritual duties of the parish. The positions were mostly filled by royal civil servants or by diocesan officials; such sinecures were convenient ways of paying them. A medieval example is William of Wykeham, first a clerk of the works on royal buildings, then a royal financial administrator, partly paid by the Bromyard portion, and eventually Lord Privy Seal, Bishop of Winchester, and Lord Chancellor. In the late 18th and early 19th centuries, both George Cope and William Cooke were portioners before helping appoint themselves vicar.

Three Mills was the manorial water corn mill, possibly the mill mentioned in Domesday Book. After the diocese gave up ownership about 1857 it eventually became part of the Buckenhill estate. The last miller and farmer, Thomas Mason, moved away in the 1870s and concentrated on his High Street corn dealing business and Richard Phipps of Buckenhill, a rich brewer from Nottingham and a great benefactor to the town, rebuilt the picturesque old mill as a pumping station and had water pumped from there to Firs Orchard and Flaggoner's Green. The water in fact came from springs on the Downs.

The pumping station was replaced in 1965 by one at Knightwick.

ST PETER'S SCHOOL AND THREE MILLS

On the 1902 and 1928 25" OS map the whole site is shown as Pumping Station and Water Works; the Mill Race and the Mill Pond, just east of the Leominster railway, are still shown coming down from the north. They left the Frome at a weir and sluice at Instone Bridge on the Tenbury road. Curiously they are not shown on the original 1885 map.

In around 1870 there were occasional Nonconformist baptisms in the mill pool.

"NATURE'S BAPTISMAL POOL"

12. OLD ROAD

Old Road is indeed one of the oldest in the town, as can be seen by the fact that at several points it verges on being a "sunken road", one so worn into the ground that it has banks on either or at least one side. It was always the road to the next important parish and minster to the west, Leominster. The name is not old though; into the 20th century it was called "Sheep Street", even by the Royal Commission on Ancient Monuments in 1932. This name was of course after the animals whose market was held at the town end of the road till some time at the end of the 19th. Much earlier, "Croxewall Streete" had continued indefinitely. In 1733 both names were used in a document about William Barnes's quarter of an acre burgage holding. By 1767 John and William Jenks were free burgesses for their properties in Sheep Street. In 1735 the borough court ordered John Hill to repair the "causeway" in front of his orchard in Sheep Street.

The burgage lots stretched further out from the centre of the town than in most Bromyard streets; on the south side, up to the field called The Clover (where Clover Road now is), on the north side not so far. James Tonkin noted that "the older houses remaining are parallel to the street and seem to show less pressure on space here than in the centre of the town." Examples are the row leading up to Bridle Cottage, no. 20, begun before 1739, as surviving documents show.

In the late 1960s Phyllis Williams had letters from two people who still remembered the sheep market in the street; Mr. Madders said that "boys used to plague the sheep and encourage them to jump over the hurdles, which when they did there were shouts of delight", and Miss Annie Roberts that "The hurdles were put under the windows of the houses, from the houses to the pavement. When not in use they were kept in the White House yard." Not surprisingly, in the first sanitary inspection of the town in 1850 for the new national General Board of Health, Sheep Street was found to be "pre-eminent among the streets of Bromyard for its unhealthiness."

At one stage there was a parcel of land on the south side, formerly part of Collington Croft, which had on its south side a brickyard with a frontage on New Road.

There were always some rather poor people in Sheep Street; in the early 1820s a Mr. Williams owed the surgeon and physician Mr. Delabere Walker £7. 10.0, and "had his bill of £7 10. 0. discharged by hauling coal in a barrow". And in 1900 George Lewis, a baker and grocer, was in debt to the extent of being brought before the Worcester bankruptcy court.

Sadly, in October 1915 Jeanette Madden, wife of a soldier, was charged at the Bromyard Police Court with being blind drunk in Sheep Street whilst in charge of two children under the age of seven. PC Prosser stated that he saw the defendant drunk. Her two children were hanging onto her dress. He told her that she was drunk, and that he would have to lock her up. She replied 'You lock me up; it would take twenty such as you'. He got her to the police station with assistance. The police had had numerous complaints about her and had asked the publicans not to supply her with drink but she acquired this by private means. They advised her to take the pledge and fined her 5s, but if she came before them again she would be sent to gaol without the option of a fine.

The early 19th century no. 12 is Grade 2 listed because: "it is a good-quality building with elaborate architectural details such as the door case and bay window; the principal elevation is particularly well-preserved, retaining much historic fabric; and it has group value with other neighbouring buildings". It shares a chimney stack at either end of the pitched roof with the adjacent buildings. These have blocked windows on the first floor; possibly because of the Window Tax which was not lifted till 1851, after a campaign based on health reasons; the great reformer Harriet Martineau called it a "tax on fresh air, sunshine, and health". It had been introduced in 1696, to help pay for William III's wars; it replaced the old Hearth

Tax, presumably on the grounds that those who could afford higher taxes could be more fairly assessed on windows than on hearths.

1937 CORONATION CELEBRATION

On the south side, nos. 1-3 and 29 are timber-framed and Grade 2 listed. The trim Roman Catholic Church and Presbytery are largely due to the hard work of Father Brislane who came as Parish Priest in 1947. The first mass in the new church was the Midnight Mass of 1956. Nos. 35 to 43 are of stone with brick dressings, much more common in Wales than in England. This must be a façade added to an earlier row of houses, because no. 35 is extensively beamed inside and there is also evidence of wattle and daub in the attic roof space. These were more burgage plots and still have the characteristic long narrow gardens.

Above them the original Conquest Theatre had a shed-like building which doubled as the Registry Office. No. 49 is another attractive old stone building aligned along the road.

The Nodens is another timber framed cottage, with a large stone chimney block and oven bulge to the street. The Nodens family lived there in the 19th century. Below it is the remains of some dry stone retaining walling; a large stone currently on the pavement shows the perils of "trace laying", that is setting the stones long side outwards and not into the wall! There is more dry stone retaining walling above The Nodens.

The Firs, no. 100, is the only grand house in Old Road, Grade II Listed. It was begun in the 17th century, built of the local Old Red Sandstone rubble (St. Maughans Formation), and fronted with brick about 1800. It has a pediment with a lunette window and Doric stone columns or pilasters; and extensive later additions to the rear from 1896.

The Revd. John Booth, incumbent of Wacton and Stanford Bishop, a member of the lesser gentry for whom the clerical profession provided a reasonable living, moved there by 1871 from Sherford House in Sherford Street. He was a bachelor and his unmarried sister lived with him. The energetic Henry Barneby at Bredenbury Court waged war against such lax clergy, and wrote: 'Old Booth used to walk to his church, see the clerk there, twirl his stick, say "no one coming to church I suppose" and walk away.' His only distinction was to have published a collection of epigrams "ancient and modern". It was reviewed rather sniffily in the Spectator.

Beyond it, no. 110, now Inglewood but originally Firs Cottage, dates partly from 1633. The mortared stone wall to the road is worth a glance: the middle part is Carboniferous period Forest gritstone, from Black Mountain Quarries at Pontrilas; the uphill and extreme downhill part, like the house, is local Old Red Sandstone rubble, mostly recently recycled from older walls. One of the Forest stones has a strange surface where grains having dissolved under pressure have recrystallized along a joint.

13. TENBURY ROAD

Tenbury Road, like so many other Bromyard streets, has changed its name more than once. The earliest form, in the *Red Book* of about 1285, was *vicus de la lone*. It had then seven full burgages, two with an extra half, eight half burgages, and two three quarter burgages plus one "parcel". This made it one of the shorter streets of the town. Later, by the time of the *Swithun Butterfield* survey of 1575, it had become Mylborowe Lane, with 16¾ burgages instead of 13½. 1½ burgages had belonged to the chantry of the Blessed Mary and were still in the hands of the Crown. One burgage belonged to Anthony Hardwick who had a considerable estate on the north side of the town; this remained in the Hardwick family till 1755. Later again, and well into the 20th century, the street was called Milvern Lane, or sometimes "Road", with the occasional variation of "Millbourne Lane" or Milborough Street, and suggestions that this was because it led to the mill at Instone Bridge.

It was the site of the horse fair and led to the "fayre cross" where Lower Hardwick Lane joins Tenbury Road, probably a marketing place for the district before the town was founded in the 1120s. After the railway reached Bromyard in 1878 there were calls for a stock market to supplement those at Hereford and Tenbury, and a meeting to establish one was called in 1887. It developed in the Milvern Lane area, because the White Horse had always been associated with stock sales and in 1888 the Worcester auctioneer John Hillman opened a sale yard by the Milvern Lane building behind the White Horse. In 1890 Sampson's doubled their sales there from monthly to fortnightly. Bentley, Hobbs & Mytton also established themselves on the east side of the road and from 1893 were announcing that the "sale will commence with arrival of the 12.15 train". On the other side of the road Arthur Griffiths and Son established themselves. In 1899 Ralph Knight bought Sampson's and built a shelter over the cattle ring. He was succeeded in the Smithfield auctioneering business by Freeman Morris and in 1925

Bentley Hobbs and Mytton expanded by buying Morris's business. They were still in business in 1970, when they were holding big sales under both names, and their name can still be seen on the wall between the Co-op and Legge's. In 1930 plans for a new stock market in Milvern Road were approved by the Urban District Council.

MILVERN LANE TOLL GATE AND TURNPIKE HOUSE

There was a turnpike on the road in the 18th century, where Firs Lane now joins it. In 1787 the tolls of Milvern Lane and Sifton Gate were set to William Hyde at an annual rent of £43, the least of the various tolls, so presumably the road to Tenbury was the least used of the various toll roads leading out of the town. The location of Sifton Gate is now uncertain. By 1813 the annual rent was £81, but still less than for the other roads. In the 1851 and 1861 censuses a toll collector was living on the spot, in 1861 the only householder with a living in servant (his niece), but there is no toll collector in 1871 so presumably the turnpike had gone.

There was a "Brick Clamp" or kiln in the road. Curiously, its exact spot is not mentioned in the 25 inch very detailed Ordnance Survey map of 1885. It had been an orchard belonging to Alfred Green of Great Malvern, shoemaker, and Thomas Devereux, of an old family in the neighbourhood. When Thomas died in 1856 his eldest son and heir Charles William Devereux of the city of Worcester, gentleman, and Green, sold this in July 1858 for £150 together with "several dwelling houses and lands in Milvern Lane" to Richard Oseman Smith of Mount Pleasant, Bromyard Down, farmer and gentleman, who had bought and inherited from Richard Oseman of Bromyard, timber dealer, other land in that part of the town. Richard Oseman had erected nine "tenements or dwelling houses" on half an acre, four by 1833, by when he had in the area a total of 22 houses, gardens and premises in the brickyard. Richard Oseman Smith, senior, passed it to his son, Richard Oseman Smith, junior, of Ashfields, Hereford Road, in 1904. This son sold some of this land and building to the County Council in 1928 for £65 at the beginning of the attempt at slum clearance.

Censuses from 1841 show that Milvern Lane with Brick Clamp was one of the poorer streets in the town, both from the occupations of the inhabitants and from the numbers of people in each house. When Benjamin Babbage surveyed the public health of the town in 1850, Milvern Lane not surprisingly was among the worst drained. A "primitive contrivance" coped with the sewerage for five houses. When the vicar, The Revd. T. Nash Stephenson, made notes in the 1870s about his needy parishioners, he recorded that among the 36 houses in Milvern Lane including "Brick Lump", nine were on the dole (a parish charity I think) A further seven were noted as "p.p", which either means "paupers", a recognised category of people in those days of the New Poor Law, or "parish payments". The charity was carefully controlled: it was for poor persons of good character of the labouring class – their children had to have been born in wedlock and they would be struck off if they were convicted of poaching, felony, or drunkenness.

In 1889 the Rural Sanitary Agency called attention to Brick Clamp, saying they had "never seen houses in such a state". Two years later the census showed that Brick Clamp was occupied by four households, one by George Haynes, a "general labourer" of 35, his wife Caroline, a machinist of 38, and eight children, Albert and George, 16 and 14, working as agricultural labourers, Emily and Henry being at school, and four younger children, Florence being 7 months. William Piper and his wife had a lodger, a labourer like Piper. Edward Jones was a gardener with four sons in work and a lodger. Henry James, a painter of 24, lived on his own. Ten years later the Haynes family were in Sheep Street, in a house where George's parents had taken in boarders and now taking them themselves. George was now working for himself at home as a cooper, as was Emily as seamstress – Henry was a bricklayer's labourer and one of the younger children had died. The house was apparently no. 12; if the existing 12 Old Road it is difficult to see how it can have normally accommodated 14 people.

In the 1901 census there were four households in what it called "Bricklamp": one headed by William Piper, now a widower of 81, with two boarders, a middle aged woman and a young baker; one by Charlotte Taylor, a young widowed tailoress with five children; one by Edward Jones, a young chemist's porter, with a brother, a sister, a niece and a nephew; the fourth by William Lock, a young house painter with a wife and five children. Charlotte Taylor was still there in 1911, with two sons, two daughters, a nephew, and an illegitimate grandson. Harriet Tylor, a spinster of 68, lived on her own. William Lock and his wife now had 8 children living with them, one away, and had lost one child in their 15 years of marriage. The fourth household was headed by Frederick James "ironmonger – porter" with a wife and four children from their ten years of marriage.

In 1899 the *News and Record* were commenting on the poor reputation of Milvern Lane and Sheep St, Bromyard, and in August 1912 here was a survey on the reported condition of two houses in

Milvern Lane. The owners were given notice that if sanitary requirements were not carried out within 7 days a closing order would be made. This was followed in December by the Medical Officer of Health ordering these two houses in Milvern Lane (and four in Sheep Street and one house in Pump Street) to be closed as unfit for human habitation.

MILVERN LANE

In 1921 the Medical Officer was favouring a Milvern Lane redevelopment scheme and the Ballhurst estate was bought by the Council for replacement housing. In 1928 a house in Milvern Street was required to install WCs.

At a council meeting in May 1932 it was asked how it was that a house in Milvern Lane was still being occupied when it had been condemned. The Medical Officer understood all the people in the house were ill. The surveyor was to inspect and report which he did the next month; the rent was 2/- per week. In 1927 the roof of a cottage fell in.

In 1936 twelve dwelling houses in Milvern Lane and four adjoining occupied dwelling houses in Brickclamp together with outbuildings were bought by the council. They were bounded on the north by premises known as Smithfield, Milvern Lane, owned and occupied by Messrs Griffiths, Auctioneers, Worcester, on the south by a warehouse and garden occupied by Messrs Bellows, Leominster, and Miss Margaret Jones, on the east by Milvern Lane, and on the west by a garden and orchard owned respectively by Miss M. Jones and the executors of Miss M. Woodhouse. On 1 July 1936 the Ministry of Health countersigned and sealed Slum Clearance Orders made by the Bromyard UDC in Little Hereford Street; the Kings Arms, Sheep Street, and nos. 14-25 Milvern Lane.

In March 1938 the Bromyard UDC prepared to receive tenders for the erection of 28 houses with roads and sewers on the Ballhurst estate to replace these derelict properties but with the approach and outbreak of war the site remained waste until after victory in 1945 when the second phase of the Ballhurst estate was built; several houses there and in Milvern Lane were finished by July 1946.

Not everything ceased with the war; in 1943 the Bromyard UDC were considering a "Housing of the working classes post war programme", and between May 1943 and September 1944 purchased, or considered purchasing, land for new council houses in various parts of the town, including land in Tenbury Road from the Misses James of Park House.

14. FIRS LANE

Firs Lane is surely the most peculiar road in Bromyard. It has a definite beginning on Tenbury Road and a definite end at the top of Old Road; but in between it is a collection of disjointed sections on some of which a car can be driven, at times a footpath, and tweaked by roads crossing it. There are houses numbered 1 to 7, odd, at the bottom, and 102-142, mostly even, in two separate bits at the top, all with the same postcode, HR7 4BA, though Firs Orchard which crosses it is HR7 4BB. Sat Navs must get baffled!

It is an old lane, possibly the boundary between Cruxwell Field to the south and Plegeliate Field to the north before the common open fields were enclosed. It is probably older than its name; The Firs at the top end is a house with a core dating from the 17th century, and a brick façade with stone dressings of about 1800; it faces very certainly onto Old Road. On the oldest Ordnance Survey map, 1831-3, the lane starts at the east end at a turnpike on Milvern Lane (Tenbury Road), and The Firs is prominently marked at the west. The kink that end does not appear, but is clear on the Tithe Map of 1844.

On that map, the first block on the south at the east end is shown to be part of the non-titheable town area of Bromyard. Where Winslow begins there is a sudden rise onto the higher ground or knapp. This is an Anglo-Saxon word and quite common in Herefordshire: Ledbury for example also has a Knapp. The great and immensely detailed OS map of 1885 notes "3 f[ee]t R[oot of] H[edge]" running south along the town boundary. The southern part of Wye Avenue runs, I think along this former boundary. West of Wye Avenue the current metalled road continues right and north to garages, but the original line is kept to by a footpath bearing slightly left and up.

In 1844 the two fields to the south of what's now that footpath are part of the small Ballhurst Farm, an "arable orchard" and then a "grass orchard". North of the lane on the Tithe Map is the arable

Quarry Field, the quarry still shown on the 1904 OS map as if it were still in use. The site must be somewhere just past the end of Frome Close.

The present footpath on the line of the old lane now runs up to the playing fields, and one can cross slightly south of the original line to where York Road and Lodon Road have a barrier to prevent driving straight through. The playing fields were Old Orchard and Nap Orchard in 1844, and there is a document of 1796 in the Local History Centre archives referring to "meadow and pasture enclosed out of Cruxwell Field now planted with fruit trees."

North of the lane, apparently on the site of Firs Court, was the reservoir to which water was pumped up from Three Bridges, and from which a windmill and water wheel pumped water to a higher reservoir at Flaggoners Green. "Early in 1927" wrote Joan Leese in the chapter on "The Parish Pump, 1850-1960" in the 1970 "*Bromyard, A Local History*", "the Knapp residents complained of the noise caused by that poor unsuitable windmill in Firs Lane, and the Council decided to sell it. But apparently there were no takers, for when there was a violent storm two years later, in December, the *Bromyard News and Record* reported that the windmill had broken loose 'and has been sailing round ever since.'". The reservoir passed out of use when the Rural and Urban District Councils joined together in 1960 to make the reservoir on the Downs.

In living memory there were no houses north of the lane; as Keith Handley remembered shortly before his sad death, the area was "just open fields belonging to Rossers at Dry Thistle Farm" which "was a lot larger in those days and supplied a great deal of the bottled milk to Bromyard families. I used to help in the dairy washing the bottles, one of which I have at home." He would have used the lane which is now the west part of Firs Orchard, but which was an early track leading to the farm. He also remembered that "at the bottom end of [Firs Road] was the "black circle" which was the cattle lorry wash down area opposite the market."

Firs Orchard leaves Old Road across what was "Orchard by house" on the Tithe Map; it has caused a small but odd kink in Firs Lane, the old straight line of the lane now being enclosed within a garden fence. Beyond that are 102-126, and then the top of Firs Lane is reached by a slightly sunken path, leading to the final metalled kink to Old Road, above which sit nos. 134-42. A footpath carries on west, as it did when it divided Lower Thorn Meadow from Lower Calves Meadow.

Some of the land of the Firs Estate was sold in 1878 to the Worcester Dwellings Improvement and Land Company. This was the real beginning of the expansion of the town onto the high slope above the shelf on which the town began.

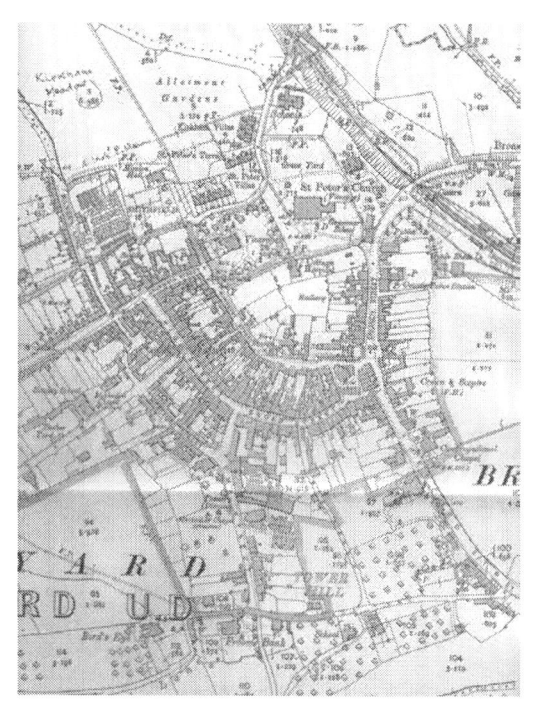

OS MAP 1885

15. LINTON LANE

Before closing this series, we really must look at a quiet byway which can claim to be one of the oldest roads in the area – perhaps *the* oldest. Linton Lane is as fine an example of a hollow way as you can find. That means that generations of people and beasts wore a track deep into the hillside. For nine hundred years the road from Worcester, once it has crossed the Frome by ford or bridge, has swung right up Sherford Street into the town; but 9,000 years ago? Or 90,000?

Undoubtedly a very old trackway followed Linton Lane up the hill. Where Highwell Lane and Nunwell Road diverge, it may have gone both ways, as public footpaths today follow each fork – perhaps one towards Hereford, one towards Leominster – or whatever was the goal before even these towns and their church centres existed. One road into mid Wales, one towards south Wales?

The right hand lane (roughly Nunwell Road today) passed between a small field called Little Holditch which was pasture on the tithe map of 1844 and a larger field which was meadow then and went up to the pre-New Road main way to Hereford, up Holditch. It followed the boundary between Bromyard and Linton. According to Phyllis Williams, much of the old hollow ways were filled in with spoil about 1936 when the Lower Westfield houses were built, and of course the even later bypass makes it extremely difficult to envisage the whole area in earlier times.

The left hand lane (Highwell Lane) forks again, and the public footpath up the right fork is again recognisably a hollow way. In 1844 the three small fields to the north were known collectively as Hayling's Orchard, though the central one seems actually to have been pasture.

FLAGGONERS GREEN TOLLHOUSE

When turnpike roads came in in the mid-18th century Linton Lane was not improved to that standard. A toll house, still standing, was erected the further side of Petty Bridge, and the road on to "Herefordshire Lake in the parish of Whitbourne" was among those mentioned in the Act of Parliament of 1751 as to be repaired. At the western ends of the lane were the Piccadilly and Flaggoners Green toll houses on the roads to Ledbury, Hereford, and Leominster.

There is a considerable amount of old retaining wall along the lane, some looking as though it may originally have been dry stone work.

What of the name "Linton"? There are several places of this Anglo-Saxon name in the country, including one near Ross-on-Wye. Most of these are thought to be the *tūn*, the homestead or village, either where flax (*līn*) grew, or by a lime tree (*lind*). Also possible is the *tūn* by a *hlinc*, either "a bank separating strips of arable land on a slope", or a (rocky) ledge. The earliest spelling, Matilda de Lynton, in the *Red Book* of about 1285, has a "y", and the Devon river Lyn and towns of Lynton and Lynmouth come from an Anglo-Saxon river name, *hlynn*, a torrent. This is not suitable for the peaceful Frome, and there was a marked preference among Anglo-Norman scribes for spelling "i" words with "y"- the *Red Book* has "skynnere", "dyche", "taylour", "Wyneslowe", for skinner, ditch, tailor, Winslow.

At the bottom of Linton Lane, the most likely site of the original *tūn*, stood the fine timber-framed Bridge Inn, a building with the date 1571 on a tie-beam. The earliest known landlord was Benjamin Palmer, who paid 15/- in the Land Tax of 1812. Seven years later, when the Napoleonic War no longer had to be paid for, his successor James Baggott only paid 12/-. Baggott, who was also a "Skinner and Wool Dealer, Dealer and Chapman", went bankrupt in 1821 and his effects, including brewing utensils, were sold by auction. The "Capital and well-accustomed INN" (with its "Piece of Hop-ground") was also put up for sale.

Samuel Gwinn ran it in 1823 but it was soon sold again and the owner, George Kelsey, put in 30 year old George Clewer to run it as an inn and posting house. By 1835 Thomas Price had taken over. In the 1851 census he was 50, victualler, farmer, and coach proprietor. He was born in Grendon, his younger wife Eliza in Hampton Charles, and they were helped by a son of 19, William, and four servants, one of whom was a nephew. In 1858 the Royal Mail coaches left the inn for Worcester at 10.30 in the morning, and for Leominster and Presteigne at 5.30 in the afternoon.

THE BRIDGE INN, LINTON LANE

In 1861 the licensee was Thomas Redding, who was also a builder. His teenage sons were a carpenter and a blacksmith, and to judge from where his seven children were born he and his wife had moved around a bit, Worcester, Suckley, Knightwick, and Whitbourne where his wife had been born. There were no living in servants, only a young lodger, Edwin Halsey, was there at the end of the decade, and soon after it lost its licence.

One final "publican" appears in the 1871 census, a young bachelor with the odd name of Armel G. Allen, with four servants and two lodgers. He was the son of a Worcester glover, and perhaps had money, because he went to a private boarding school in Worcester. He is completely untraceable thereafter, and may have emigrated to the United States.

The inn seems to have closed by the end of the decade. The fine timber framed building is still there, now a private dwelling. There were cottages opposite it, perhaps at one stage the "Talbot" tavern, which had to be demolished when the bypass was built.

Higher up the lane, on the south side, was the school built in the 1870s at the expense of the Nonconformist tanner Mr. Jenks as the "British" school, that is, under the auspices of the British and Foreign School Society for the Education of the Labouring and Manufacturing Classes of Society of Every Religious Persuasion. Its previous premises in the Friends Meeting House behind Broad Street did not comply with the Education Act of 1870. In 1922 the boys moved to join St. Peter's School in Church Lane, and the town's "infants" moved to Linton Lane. The school closed in 1965, and was used for a time by the Scouts and other voluntary bodies. In 1995 Mr. and Mrs A. Jenkins had a house built on the site by the Border Oak Co., "using traditional techniques".

LINTON LANE SHOWING THE BRITISH SCHOOL

Frog Lane went through to Linton Lane before the bypass. Bishall House, no. 12, is all that remains of Bishall Terrace. Another former feature of the lane was a coal yard, from 1950 to 2000, when that too was replaced by a house.

FROME BANK

The final feature of Linton Lane is Frome Bank. The original house was built by a solicitor, William West, who lived there till his death in 1880. His spinster daughters and Worcester wine merchant son then sold it, and in 1901 it was lived in by William Holland, the grandson of the novelist, Elizabeth Gaskell by her daughter Marianne, of Birchyfields and Alfrick Court.

In 1905 it was bought by Cadbury's of Birmingham as a convalescent home for their young women workers. The first arrived in September 1906.

Immediately on the outbreak of war in August 1914 it was offered to the War Office as a hospital and accepted. Among the first wartime residents were wounded Belgians that December. Later photographs show about 30 soldiers; they had hospitality from locals, as some pictures are in the grounds of Sherford House, or at a tea party at Tower Hill. A troupe of teenage girls in fancy dress came in to entertain them on at least one occasion. The temporary hospital closed smartly at the end of the war, and Cadbury's went on using it till 1935. An Infant Welfare Clinic was inaugurated there in 1928, which was held "every stock market Thursday" for children under 5.

The old house then had some thirty years as a children's home, and may have taken evacuees in World War 2. Miss E. Morris was matron for 16 years until 1955.

The Bromyard GP Dr. Philip Crosskey worked tirelessly from 1982 to 1989 with an Action Committee to get a new Community Hospital built on the site – the only hospital in the town then was the former workhouse, Linton Hospital. This had gradually mutated over the years, through its 1940 description as a 'Public Assistance Institution' to its incorporation in the new National Health Service in 1948. In 1955 the Birmingham Regional Hospital Board decided to spend £16,000 on modernising the building, carried out in 1957. In 1959 the *News & Record* observed that "To many, the hospital was still thought of as a workhouse, but this is a very wrong idea. A great deal of work and alterations have been done. There were new wards and new equipment."

The existing Community Hospital at Frome Bank opened in 1988.

FURTHER READING

Phyllis Williams, *Bromyard - Minster, Manor and Town*, 1987 – available from BDLHS

Jean Hopkinson, *Where have all the Courts gone?* 2003– available from BDLHS

Duncan James, *An analysis of the historic fabric of fifty buildings in the central area of Bromyard* 2009 - available from BDLHS

Bromyard's Victorian Heritage – a book of Photographs - available from BDLHS

E D Pearson, *Two Churches: Two Communities, Bromyard and Stanford Bishop* - available from BDLHS

J. Eisel, and R. Shoesmith, *The Pubs of Bromyard, Ledbury and East Herefordshire,* Logaston Press 2003.

Bromyard, A Local History, ed. Joseph G. Hillaby and Edna Pearson, 1970 – out of print, available in BDLHS library

The BDLHS archives include old photographs, photocopies and microfiches of parish registers for Bromyard and surrounding parishes together with many books, articles, and other documents on the town and area's history. There are also copies, on film, of the local newspaper, *The Bromyard News & Record* from 1883 – 1970, and of subsequent local papers to date. For more details see: www.bromyardhistorysociety.org.uk/archive1

The Herefordshire Archive and Record Centre (HARC) at Rotherwas has many original documents for Bromyard and surrounding parishes including the two surveys of the bishops's estates, the *Red Book* of around 1285 and *Swithun Butterfield's* of 1578.

An Interesting Guide to Streets in Bromyard

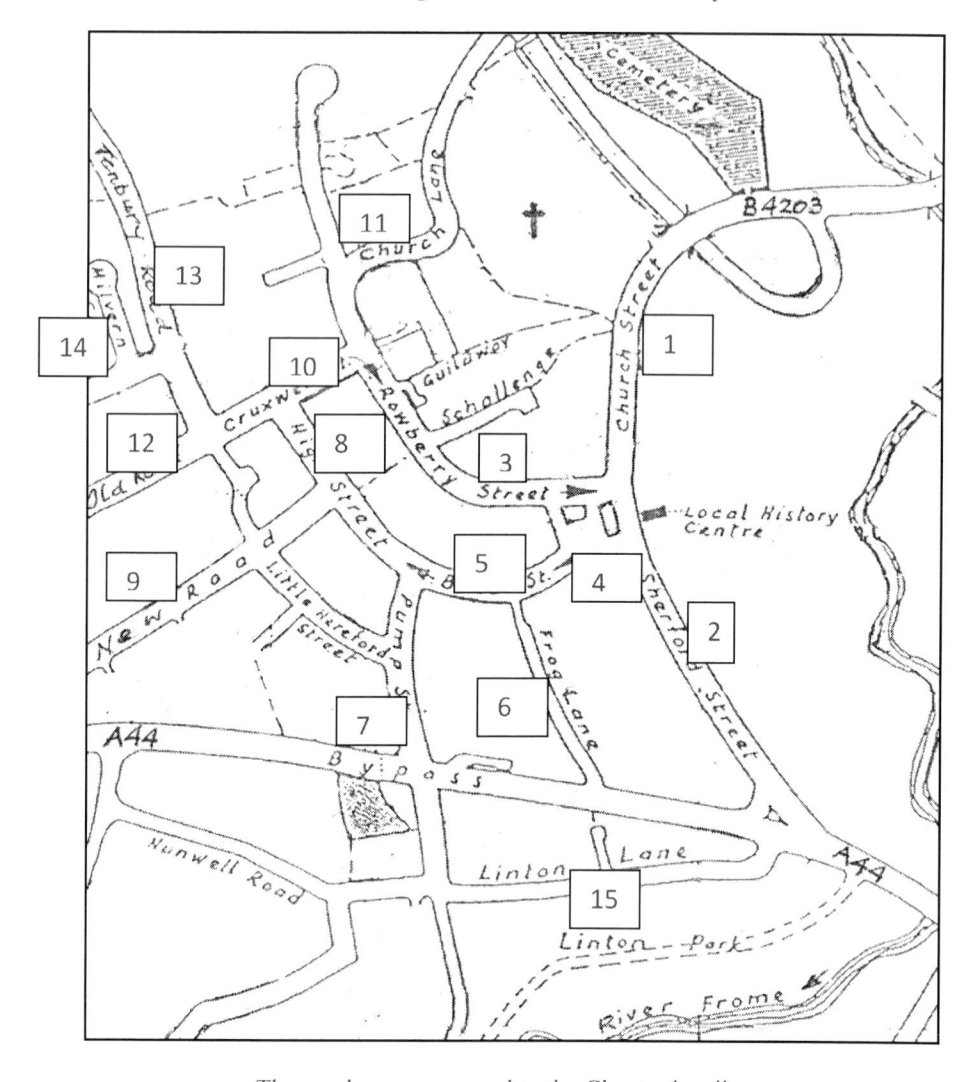

The numbers correspond to the Chapter headings

1. Church Street
2. Sherford Street
3. Rowberry Street
4. Market Square
5. Broad Street
6. Frog Lane
7. Pump Street and Tower Hill
8. High Street
9. New Road
10. Cruxwell Street
11. Church Lane
12. Old Road
13. Tenbury Road
14. Firs Lane
15. Linton Lane

Made in the USA
Columbia, SC
21 March 2018